The Mentor in Me: What To Do & What Not To Do

Cover design by Patti Knoles
http://virtualgraphicartsdepartment.com

Book layout by The Formatting Formula
www.formattingformula.com

ISBN: 978-0-9983277-0-9

Because of the dynamic nature of the Internet, any web addresses or links contained in this book may have changed since publication and may no longer be valid. The views expressed in this work are solely those of the author and do not necessarily reflect the views of the publisher, and the publisher hereby disclaims any responsibility for them.

The author of this book does not dispense medical advice or prescribe the use of any technique as a form of treatment for physical, emotional, or medical problems without the advice of a physician, either directly or indirectly. The intent of the author is only to offer information of a general nature to help you in your quest for emotional and spiritual well-being. In the event you use any of the information in this book for yourself, which is your constitutional right, the author, and the publisher assume no responsibility for your actions.

www.writestreampublishing.com

CONTENTS

Foreword by Bob Proctor   IV

Foreword

October 21, 2016. Toronto, Canada office of The Proctor Gallagher Institute

Shortly after I awoke this morning I received a text from Pat Barry, a well-known broadcaster in the United States. I could hear his voice as I read the message. "Good Morning Bob. Fifty-five years ago today the #1 song was *Hit the Road Jack* by Ray Charles. That same day, Bob Dylan recorded his first album; the total cost was $400. It was also the day it all started for you. Thank God that happened! Happy Anniversary Bob and many thanks for all your help."

You see it was on October 21, 1961, that Ray Stanford put Napoleon Hill's *Think and Grow Rich* into my hands and my whole life began to change. This morning's text message was a reminder that my success journey started with a mentor and a book. So, I felt it very apropos to start the Foreword to William's book...*The Mentor in Me* on this date.

If Ray had not given me the direction that he did, I would not have had the success that I have enjoyed, and I could not have offered William direction in the way that I did.

The lessons I offered William were like a mathematical formula that another mentor shared with me way back in the mid-1960's. Leland Val Van de Wall came into my life at a critical time. My life had already changed dramatically from reading *Think and Grow Rich* and I was trying to figure out why...what had happened. Val said, "Bob, when a change takes place in a person's life, it is actually a shift in awareness."

He explained how centuries ago a very wise King Solomon said, "In all your getting, get understanding."

Val went on to explain that what I was seeking to understand is that there is a process that we go through as life unfolds. The process involves **Seven Levels of Awareness**. As we progress from one level to the next, so our world also changes. Val talked about how we begin our lives in an animalistic state where we are totally dependent on others. We can stay stuck at that first level or we can progress. If we work through all the lessons in the **Seven Levels of Awareness**, we will end up becoming a master of ourselves. When we accomplish mastery, we will find that we have also developed a meaningful relationship with God. Val is the man I give credit to for laying these seven levels out for me so clearly. He was a brilliant person and a wonderful friend. He certainly was an enlightened individual.

I have invested fifty-five years studying every day what Val, Ray Stanford, Napoleon Hill, and other mentors shared with me and the past two decades sharing with William what I learned.

When William initially asked if I would mentor him, I told him I would spend time with him and that I would suggest various things he could do. If he did them, he would eventually be led to the mentor that resides within. And now William has decided to do what I have done, share what he has learned. And you are the beneficiary.

William has laid out the **Seven Levels of Awareness** like a master astrologer charting the planets. He has done an outstanding job of journaling the lessons he learned over the years and how he learned them. You will find as you work through the levels that you can relate to many of the lessons. As you go from chapter to chapter you will become aware of the various levels of awareness; where your life may have been a puzzle, the awareness you develop will bring clarity to your mind.

If you give *The Mentor in Me* serious thought, it's going to do for you what my mentors did for me. You'll also begin to reap the many personal and financial benefits that William has enjoyed because of the growth he has experienced.

The *Mentor in Me* is not a book that you pick up and read. It's a book you form a relationship with and you study daily for the rest of your life.

Bob Proctor

Acknowledgements

The seed, which became this book, was planted at The Matrixx Event, August 2015 in Toronto, Canada; an event hosted by the Proctor Gallagher Institute. Bob Proctor and his business partner, Sandy Gallagher extended a special invitation to me to attend that life-changing week. It is one more reason I am forever grateful to the ultimate Mentor, Bob Proctor. His guidance and counsel over the past two decades can only be explained as an ever-unfolding life raft, one I have used many times to reach safe harbor. Bob's friendship and patience has been a torch of hope and calmness of mind over the years and I intend to spend the rest of my life paying it forward to those who desire a better life and better results and to those who choose to unleash their own hidden powers. I am honored to carry Bob Proctor's principles forward.

Unending thanks to my loving wife, Deborah, who has participated in and witnessed my transformation. Providence prevailed the day we met — you are my muse and constant reminder of what is good and right.

Many thanks go to my long-time business associate, good friend, and mentor Marty Jeffery who added to this book as only his genius can do. His authoring of the Epilogue is a perfect finish to this first installment.

To my family, for their love, support and guidance which led me to first understand the power of mentoring.

Thank you, Patti Knoles, who designed the book cover; the all-so-talented Canadian editor, Elizabeth Collins. To our IT team in Denver, Colorado at HIVE Digital Strategy — you are the best!

To my publisher, Writestream Publishing. I am proud to be associated with you.

And finally, I want to acknowledge you, the reader. May your journey through the Levels of Awareness be met with much joy, happiness, and success. Please remember that the most important aspect of raising your awareness is repetition: Hold on. Don't let go. Just trust the process.

William V. Todd

Introduction

The source of this book

Change is inevitable. Those three words are under, in, and around everything my mentor has believed in and taught for over fifty years. Bob Proctor is the 'last man standing' in many ways. He is a teacher, a motivator, a speaker, and an author. He is a Master.

Bob's hero and mentor, Earl Nightingale, was one of the giants in the self-improvement movement. Beginning with the teachings of Thomas Troward, Emerson, and the genius of William James, these mentor/guides made the change that is inevitable into something we could manage — something that could catapult us into a much more meaningful and successful reality. They held onto the truth until it became their character, their life's work as a mentor. These giants brought about a vast shift in the way we think, the way we see the world, ourselves, and others. We (you and I) are the custodians of the lessons and the legacies these mentors laid down. Their lessons are the source of this book.

> *"If you can change your mind, you can change your life."*
> *- William James*

Bob Proctor wasn't my first mentor, however. Mr. Grimes, my fourth-grade teacher was. Mr. Grimes introduced me to the idea of taking a concept from design through to manufacturing, marketing, and sales. Our class project involved a Nerf-type basketball and backboard. Mr. Grimes instilled in me the importance of team work and service and the value of completing a worthwhile project.

My father was also a great mentor; he taught me about bouncing back from adversity and about never giving up.

But despite having great mentors in my childhood, as an adult I just couldn't put it all together or at least keep it all together. Every time there was a change – in the economy, in the industry, in my relationships... all that I had worked so hard to improve on, turned into failure...until I met Bob Proctor.

When Bob agreed to mentor me, he knew that his primary job as a mentor was to bring out the mentor in me. Only then would I have a chance at achieving sustainable success. He was like a smarter, older brother who continued to teach and care for me despite my resistance. He took, and sometimes dragged me, through the **Seven Levels of Awareness**, from my primal, angry, reactive self all the way to my higher-self and my desire for Mastery. And that is what this book is about. It is a chance for you, the reader, to see firsthand the colossal messes I made before I learned that all along there were easy-to-follow, predictable laws just waiting to lift me into a level called Mastery. It is a level available to all of us. Bob reached it by studying and by being mentored by the masters who came before him and you can as well.

> *"What does your attitude proclaim to the world about you today? It is never too late to change your story, start by changing your thoughts and your attitude."*
>
> *- Bob Proctor*

It wasn't until I changed my attitude and made myself accountable and willing to work through the ***Seven Levels of Awareness*** that I could change from the person who pretended I had it all together (even though my life was falling apart) to someone who has achieved sustainable success – and not just in business but in every area of my life. I have also learned how to successfully navigate adversity. I changed back to that optimistic grade-four soul who couldn't sleep because of the excitement of working on an important project.

The principles I share in this book are more powerful than your stories of where you have been and what you have done up until now. It matters not even how many times you have failed, only that you are willing to be responsible for your growth. I will share with you what growing into success can look like and I'll give you Seven Practical Steps to make your journey a great deal smoother.

CHAPTER ONE

The 1st Level is called — Animal

This first level on the Seven Levels of Awareness is about reaction. Animals react when faced with a threatening situation — it's fight or flight. We humans do the same. Something happens and we react instinctively! A driver cuts us off in traffic and we curse at them, we don't get the promotion we were hoping for and we storm out of the office, we get our bank statement in the mail and numb ourselves with food, alcohol, or television instead of thinking of ways to get out of debt…. What does a person who has mastered their life do? They respond instead of react. It is the first step to achieving sustainable success in every area of life.

10:00 p.m. PST Portland International Airport, Portland, Oregon

When I was in my late thirties I traveled a lot for work. During one particularly busy stretch, I took three round-trip flights from Portland, Oregon to Paris, France within a ninety-day period. The flight was made even longer with a stopover in Cincinnati. On all three returns the airline lost my bag and I was the last one standing at the carousal at 10:00 pm. To make matters worse, I still had a three-hour drive to get home.

I got to know the airline's baggage attendant well — we were now on a first-name basis. The first two times my luggage was lost, we joked about it but by the third lost-luggage event my patience had reached its limit. What was an annoyance morphed into self-righteous anger and I lost it! Fueled by jet lag but more by immaturity and a sense of entitlement, I spewed out a string of reactive emotions and profanity.

The baggage attendant just stood there waiting for me to finish.

I will never forget his calm response to my explosive reaction. He said, "William, calm down. I am not the person who lost your luggage. I am the guy who will find your bag and deliver it to your front door ... just like I did the last two times."

His response stopped me in my tracks. Oh, what I would have given to have known the *Seven Levels of Awareness* back then. I could have spared this gentleman my animalistic behavior.

Bob's Handwritten Coaching Comment

william had not learned when you re-act to another person or situation you have let them control you. when you respond (think & act) you control you.

So Why Do We Still Have This Animalistic Instinct?

Understanding the purpose of the fight, freeze, flight response can lead to greater insights into our own behavior. First, it is a fact of our physiology that we react under stress, which is why it's also called *acute stress* syndrome. It is one reason that our ancient ancestors survived. It is how animals survive as well.

Animals have primal instincts like fear built into them, but we humans also have innate desires and a sympathetic nervous system as a part of the manufacturer's design. Therefore, we have the capacity to develop emotions or learned behaviors which can trigger those primal feelings of fight or flight.

> *"When you REACT, you are giving away your power.*
> *When you RESPOND, you are staying in control of yourself."*
>
> *- Bob Proctor*

William James, one of America's most distinguished early psychologists, said the sequence is: perception followed by bodily expressions followed by emotional feeling. So, we see a bear; we tremble, and we run. Some people tremble and then freeze (play dead). The idea that emotions can cause a physical reaction emphasizes the intimate relationship between our bodies and our mental state. But even though we have control over our mind, we don't always use it to control our thoughts, attitudes, and actions.

When I was a child, it was easy to find ways to keep myself in a playful and happy mood. With a national forest at my back door, I learned to explore! It always seemed to get dark too early! But as time passed and I let unhappy circumstances and my family's anger dictate my emotional state; I became angry, bitter, reactive, and blaming. And everything about life suddenly seemed dark.

As an adult, I would fake a smile and try to fool people into thinking that I was on top of the world. But inside, I was self-destructing. Was it associations or my upbringing that caused my attitude to shift from happy to angry? It was more than that.

Maslow was probably right

Maslow's theory holds that human beings are motivated by unsatisfied needs and that lower needs take precedence over higher ones. If we are stuck out in the freezing rain, we will seek shelter before eating a sandwich or thinking about how to become enlightened. When a need is mostly satisfied, it no longer motivates us and the next higher need takes its place. Under stressful conditions or when it feels like our survival is threatened, we either regress or stay stuck on a lower-need level. Some people live their entire lives feeling that their survival is threatened. When their great career falls flat, they are suddenly *driven* to find attention from their friends and loved ones. When they have family problems, it feels like love is all they ever wanted, all they ever needed. When they face bankruptcy, even when everything else in their life is good, they suddenly can't think of anything except money. Usually, however, they just get angry.

Anger [Animal] as a Survival Mechanism

We've all had anger directed at us in such a way that it causes damage to almost everyone involved. While most of us understand that anger is not a negative emotion, we are often uncomfortable expressing it. But anger can also be a force for good. Most reform happens because an individual and then a critical mass of people have become angry enough to stand up for themselves and enact change.

But becoming enraged is an entirely different matter. We are enraged when we hold on to those angry thoughts, letting them bottle up inside until we explode, wiping out everyone around us. If this anger is a learned behavior from watching our family authority figures, then not only do we have our own anger to deal with, we have our ancestors' anger manifesting as well.

That's what I experienced in my upbringing – rage that was passed down from generation to generation. I was angry with people I had never met and things I had never experienced. The feeling that there was us (my family of origin) and them (the others) made justification of this anger even easier. I saw that anger play out with both my mother and father and I was terrified that I had inherited this same curse. I did not want to have the explosive outbursts, but they happened anyway.

So here's the question:

Are you holding the people you love hostage — blaming them for your anger? Perhaps they have stopped being honest with you about their real needs fearing yet another outburst. Maybe they have developed their own resentments because they do not feel safe enough to express themselves. Or, they may have left you entirely just to get away from the constant sense of danger. The people for whom we care most about often feel so beaten down and victimized by our anger that they have to tip-toe around us. They appear weak and cowardly but they are just as angry --- and so they should be. Unfortunately, most of their anger gets mismanaged and turns into depression.

All of this will, of course, set the stage for the next generation of people to express their uncontrolled anger and the ones they live with or work with to walk on eggshells. Thankfully we have been given a solution: you no longer need to be frightened of the anger that lies within you — you can use it for self-discovery and to gain personal power. You can transmute that anger into something wonderful. The bad news? If you do not gain an upper hand on this emotion, you can never graduate to the next level of awareness.

"In every situation, there is a space between the situation and how you respond to it, and in that space, you can decide ... are you going to react or are you going to respond?"

- Bob Proctor

The Animal in Me Can't Stand the Animal in You.

One of the most interesting aspects of coaching is the amount of angry thoughts and animalistic behavior I find lurking behind the façade of a relationship. It is just as amazing to consider that many of these relationships are also suffering from *terminal uniqueness* because they believe no one else could possibly understand. During coaching sessions on relationship issues, I am often asked, "What would you know about troubled marriages where children are involved — you don't have children." This is an interesting observation but the truth is that I am an expert on failed relationships involving children. After all, I was a kid with parents who were ignorant about what was necessary for a healthy relationship. I am still able to run those childhood scenarios across the screen of my mind. I believe that I saw everything on full display as I was growing up and that created a paradigm that led to my own failed marriage. Here was my conclusion and unanalyzed law: *You stay together no matter how miserable you (or your partner) may be.* I was ignorant about how a great marriage could be.

Now please do not take the statement about my parents in the wrong way. It is not said in disrespect of the people who loved me and put a roof over my head. If you look up the definition of the word ignorant, it simply states: *lacking knowledge or awareness in general.* My parents weren't choosing the right thoughts because they didn't know there was an option. They had no awareness of what they were doing and their thoughts, anger, and attitude led me to develop some very powerful negative perceptions. For example: a primary reason I thought a couple should stay together was based on the way others might react to my failure, "What would people say?" What would the neighbors, family members, or people at church think?" Staying together wasn't for love or even growth; it was me trying to avoid what seemed like an even greater humiliation and pain. And I am not alone in that thinking.

When Bob first started mentoring me he had to repeatedly show me that there is usually some hidden benefit to becoming angry. The benefit could have been that it kept me from being totally overwhelmed by life circumstances. It might have been that I was protected from dealing with the grief or sadness that was underlying the original family-of-origin anger. It could have been that I felt entitled to my anger. But at what cost?

I am still surprised by how many individuals use affairs, alcohol, drugs, gambling, and a host of other mindless activities to distract themselves from the possibility of humiliation and pain. It's like hitting yourself in the head with a hammer to dull the pain of a headache.

I have also witnessed many who have suppressed their unhappiness to the point of becoming ill, and in some cases with serious and lasting diseases. Are you getting the point? The diseases, the addictions, and the distractions are all fueled by a lack of open and truthful communication — because of the inability to make a decision. And the decision is the start of recovery.

Every time I mentor someone on decision-making they unequivocally and unanimously say, "I can't believe I waited so long to make this decision. I am so happy and grateful now." I tell them, "Well, the ability was always within you. You just needed to understand that your deep-rooted paradigms had a grip on all your genetic coding forcing you into denial. Believing things that were passed on in your generational programing may have forced you into a *fight or flight* mindset but you now have a choice to stop and think." Or as a very wise man once said many years ago:

"The problem with people today is they simply don't think."

- *Dr. Albert Schweitzer,* Nobel Peace Prize Recipient 1952

CHANGE YOUR THOUGHTS

Do You Remember the Saying, "Mind over Matter?"

Mind over matter simply means that we have the power to create with our mind, the power to overcome adversity by using the mind -- by acting rather than re-acting. Thoughts are just things we create with our mind. We create thoughts every day of our lives. But... like trains moving through a station, we don't have to catch every one that approaches. Mind over matter means we can focus on catching the thought that will take us to where we want to go.

Merriam-Webster defines thinking as the action of using our mind to produce ideas and make decisions. But most of us let circumstances and the outside world tell us what to think; we react to sensory factors, which are like a six-lane highway during rush hour. There are literally millions of totally unrelated and useless bits of information streaming into our consciousness through our senses during our waking hours. Small wonder we go 'Animal'. And yet, we don't have to remain victims and we definitely don't have to go 'Animal'!

We aren't animal because it is not how humans were designed. We have the ability to accept or reject anything that comes to us through our senses. And unlike animals, we can use the spiritual power that is always flowing in and through us to access situation-changing ideas. We have been gifted with higher mental faculties of:

INTUITION

PERCEPTION

WILL

MEMORY

REASON

IMAGINATION

No other form of life was given all of these creative faculties. When we begin developing and effectively using them, we can control our responses to the outside world and stop letting the outside world control us. The more we use our creative faculties, the higher we move up the Ladder of Awareness and the better able we are to respond instead of react.

CHANGE YOUR ATTITUDE

But William, It's Your Attitude

One of the most over-used and misunderstood words in the English language is attitude. Managers tell their sales team that their attitude controls their sales. Counselors tell couples they need to change their attitude if they want their relationship to improve. Doctors tell patients that they have done all they can and it is up to the patient to develop a positive, healing attitude. Parents tell teenagers to get a new attitude. You might think that anything that packs this much power would be a subject we study in school. It isn't; and if you ask the next ten people you meet what attitude means, you will probably get ten different answers.

And once you have a clear understanding of what attitude is and how attitudes are formed, you realize that only a small percentage of the population are in control of their attitude. In truth, much of your attitude is being controlled by the media, other people, and the conditions and circumstances in your life. I'm not being philosophical; it is a very real problem that given your attitude has such a big effect on the quality of your life. So, let's talk about what attitude is and how you can use this information to raise your awareness and shift every aspect of your life.

"The greatest discovery of all time is that a person can change their future merely by changing their attitude."

- Oprah Winfrey

Attitude is a creative cycle that begins with our choice of thoughts. As we internalize ideas or become emotionally involved with our thoughts, we create the second stage in forming an attitude; we move our entire being – mind and body – into a new vibration. Our conscious awareness of this vibration is referred to as feelings. The mind controls feelings and ultimately dictates whether our feelings will be positive or negative by our choice of thoughts. Those thoughts then create our actions and our behavior. So, attitude is the sum of our thoughts, feelings, and actions. Attitude and results are inseparable. They follow one another like night follows day. There is a term used to describe this relationship – it is *The Law of Cause and Effect.*

As you can see, your attitude is determined by the nature of the ideas that you permit yourself to get emotionally involved in. The physical expression is automatic. It doesn't matter if the choice is conscious or unconscious. It is what it is. You can say, "I didn't know," but that's too bad, you still lose. In life, there is no allowance for ignorance. But there is good news:

Good thoughts = good feelings > which lead to good actions > which lead to good results.

Bad thoughts = bad feelings > which lead to bad actions > which leads to poor results.

Bottom line: if you think in negative terms, you will get negative results; if you think in positive terms, you will achieve positive results. Yes. It is that simple.

When Bob first mentored me, he said that attitude is directly related to the *First Level of Awareness - Animalistic.* Animals can do only three things because of their level of awareness. They can fight, flee, or freeze (play dead). If I remained ignorant, those would have remained my only choices. The saddest thing about knowing about the **Seven Levels of Awareness** is realizing the number of individuals who are stuck on that first level. They don't understand why they are angry or depressed all the time, they only know that they are angry and depressed. All the while their ignorance and negative attitude keeps the blame/anger/failure cycle in motion and they remain stuck.

> *"Attitude is the composite of your thoughts, feelings, and actions."*
>
> *- Bob Proctor*

CHANGE YOUR BEHAVIOR

Change your Behavior, Change your Life.

At any given moment, you could be facing many challenges, most of which you have absolutely no control over. However, the one thing you are one hundred percent in control of is your attitude. When you surrender control of your attitude to what appears to be a negative situation, you then react to that situation. More often than not, reacting is inappropriate.

As I mentioned, it was both a genetic and environmental history that kept me stuck in a reactive pattern of negative thoughts and poor choices. As I internalized ideas and became emotionally involved with my negative thoughts, I was creating the second stage in forming an attitude. I had created negative feelings that would move my entire being – mind and body — into a vibration bound for lousy results.

Those lousy results kept showing up in my life until I met Bob. He said I had come to a cross-road and I needed to make a decision.

At last I saw that my entire life and my results were not someone else's fault; my thoughts had led to my actions and my habitual behavior had become my character. I had to take a close look at my life. As Bob suggested; I had to evaluate the results I was creating in all areas, not just business. That's what I am asking you to do right now. Don't wait for a better time! Write it all down – the times when you have blamed others, the times when you chose negative thoughts followed by negative actions. It's hard to argue with the facts when you see it all laid out in front of you in black (or blue) and white.

I will never ever forget Bob making the following statement at a transitional point in my life. He said,

"You need to make up your mind, that right here, right now, you will choose a great attitude."

When you arrive at the conclusion that attitude is a creative cycle that begins with your choice of thoughts that affects your behavior and ultimately your life — you enter the process referred to as *The Law of Attraction.* You also reach a critical point in understanding the **First Level of Awareness** and in changing your life.

Bob's Handwritten Coaching Comment

William was letting his GENETIC CONDITIONING Control his attitude, his THOUGHTS...FEELINGS...ACTIONS which caused his results... B.

MENTOR'S MESSAGE

To this day, it's still difficult for me to take responsibility for my anger. For the most part I have learned how to use anger to enact good rather than to destroy, but each time I say that someone or something controls my old paradigms of anger, I must pause, think, and decide to bring the responsibility back to me.

I ask myself: How and where did I allow my limits to be crossed? Do I know my limits? Was I inviting someone to fail so I could take a stab at them later? Did they know what my expectations were or was I expecting them to read my mind? As I started taking responsibility for my anger, I was horrified to discover how much damage I had done to the people around me. I also had to look at what benefit my family of origin perceived from holding onto all their anger. And after a time, there it was – my family had been wronged in the past. The anger gave them the strength to survive. The benefit was clear, the anger led to endurance, to a sense of justice and fairness. It worked for them. That is, it worked until it became twisted into victimhood and rage. And until I faced their anger as well as my own, I couldn't take my power back.

If you are suffering from unresolved rage, it might be a generational learned behavior. Maybe you had an angry parent and you learned that anger was the only way to resolve issues or perhaps you couldn't express your concerns for fear of angering them even more. But at what moment did their problem become your anger? You are not a victim of your genetic disposition or your history. Taking responsibility for the anger, looking at how you might have been part of the problem, reminding yourself that you are responsible for your anger (and your expressions of it) puts the power directly back in your hands.

WHAT TO DO / WHAT NOT TO DO

1. What is your attitude right now? Remember that the first step in taking responsibility for moving past the *First Level of Awareness* is acknowledging the negative attitudes that you are holding on to. If you are unsure, choose a word or several words from the list below:

    Angry   Betrayed   Critical   Judgmental   Apathetic

    Depressed   Skeptical   Indifferent   Jealous   Resentful

    _____

    _____

    _____

    Then right here, right now, make up your mind that you will choose a great attitude.

2. Who controls your attitude? Before you respond instinctually and say "I control it" think of the times when you have allowed (and continue to allow) others to control your attitude.

    _____

    _____

    _____

3. Do you react rather respond to situations? Think of a recent situation when you reacted instead of responding. Knowing what you know now, how will you react the next time?

    _____

    _____

    _____

WORDS OF WISDOM

- Think before you speak.

- Blame is an excuse. Take responsibility for your thoughts.

- Do things that will help improve your attitude – go to the gym, breathe, read inspiring books, clear out the clutter in your home or office.

- If someone is having a bad day, give them some space. If you have friends with chronic bad attitudes, get new friends.

- If you are having a bad day, take some time out.

- Who you hang out with will ultimately reflect your attitude. Enlist the support of a mentor or friend to hold you responsible.

- Be nice. Learn to smile at every situation.

"Responsibility is a choice. I often refer to it as being the key to freedom. Your future can be everything you have ever dreamed about and then some. You have the talent and tools to experience one beautiful day after another. That is, in fact, what I believe the architect of the universe had in mind for you when you were created. If that was not so, you would have never been endowed with such awesome powers."

- Bob Proctor

CHAPTER TWO

Mass

The 2nd Level of Awareness is called — Mass

The mass population lives by a clock, run by agendas — controlled by other people. Think about it. The masses have historically gone in the wrong direction. Why is that? It is because we have been programmed to. We were taught by our parents who were taught by their parents. We were taught by teachers who were taught by their teachers.

9:00 a.m. PST Pacing the Driveway in Bend, Oregon

In early 2000, I had just turned forty-one. I had been talking to Bob about a decision I'd been putting off for years - divorce. It was one of the most difficult decisions that I would ever have to make. I had been so concerned about the impact a divorce would have on the other people in our lives that I had blinded myself to the truth. I finally admitted to myself, and to Bob, the devastation that was taking place in my mind and body from remaining in an ambivalent state. But then Bob made it crystal-clear. Not only was my ambivalence creating dis-ease in my own body, it was having a negative drag on everyone around me, including my wife. Even then, I couldn't see how I would be able move out of the mental prison I had created.

When I asked Bob what the first step should be, given that my wife and I had a heap of investments and material goods, I will never forget his simple, yet crushing counsel. "Give her everything." After collecting my lower jaw from the driveway, I informed him that he must have no idea of my net worth. He responded, "I do not care what you have, only what you can create by moving forward."

It immediately became apparent how completely ignorant and unaware I was. By not making a decision, by getting stuck on details, by not moving forward, I had created great unhappiness and stress in my life. Since that milestone event, so many people, including my former spouse, have commented on how close they thought I was to the edge of an eruption and total devastation.

> Bob's Handwritten Coaching Comment

William was learning you can only measure what you are letting go of ... you can never measure what you are going to get. He was in for a nice surprise ... B

"Once you make the decision, you will find all the people, resources and ideas you need ... every time."

- Bob Proctor

Follow the Crowd is a Signature of the Mass Consciousness Level

At the time of my separation, I had no idea about levels of awareness; I only knew I was stuck. But the way I was reacting and responding to my circumstances and how I kept trying to conform myself (and everyone else) to what was happening, which was an indicator that I was stuck at the Mass Level.

Being stuck at the *Second Level of Awareness* (Mass) was totally exhausting. It meant that I had to convert countless beings (the masses) to my way of thinking and, ultimately, my way of feeling. I don't mean manipulation for sinister or selfish reasons necessarily. Usually I just tried to get people to do what I wanted because I thought it would be good for everyone. If they would do it my way, all would be wonderful. Sadly, those who were also stuck at the Mass level, were thinking the same thing -- causing endless conflict.

In the mid-80s, I had a job as a project manager assistant for a construction company based in San Diego, California. I was responsible for a large territory and drove more than two hundred miles a day checking job-sites. My territory was from Valencia to Long Beach and Malibu to Palm Springs. Even back then Los Angeles freeways were jammed unless it was between 10 am and 2 pm. I was miserable sitting for long stretches in traffic bottlenecks and not being able to get to the job sites on time. So, the company placed me at a sub-branch near the Mojave Desert close to where a housing boom was happening and life was once again going *"my way"* as Frank Sinatra once sang. Eventually I was given the role of branch manager. I was now responsible for a fleet of trucks, an enormous warehouse, millions of dollars' worth of inventory, construction sites, and dozens of employees. As much as I loved my job, I often found myself in the center of a group of individuals who continually sucked me into their negative brainstorming sessions.

Two years into that job, I received notice of an annual evaluation. The owner of the company pulled up in his blue Ferrari and said, "William, come in to the regional manager's office and have a seat." Then, he asked, "Why do you think you have such a problem here as a project manager?" Imagine my surprise! "What? We're the most successful branch in the state." And his reply was, "Says who? Certainly not the profit and loss reports I am getting. And your evaluation reads that your attitude is one of the worst in the company." I was shocked beyond measure. I immediately fell back into an animalistic state of mind. I wanted to lash out and say, "I quit" and walk straight out of the meeting. But my need to look cool took over and I tempered my reactionary response. I ran a very tight ship and I couldn't understand what he was talking about so I said, "I don't understand? I mean, my results are impeccable: my jobs all come in on time and under budget. I feel everything's great." He said, "Your demeanor is confrontational and you're losing money on almost all of your jobs ...and you are fired."

I was angry enough to challenge him but instead, I made a decision right there and then that I would never have a job again! I took that totally adverse situation as the catalyst to begin my journey as an entrepreneur. Hopefully you will get to make your choices based in love and not fear and anger and inaccurate information (I found out later that the bookkeeper was *cooking the books* and that my branch had been profitable all along!).

But why did I have to be taken to that very bad place before I decided to become an entrepreneur? It was because I was still at the **Mass Consciousness Level of Awareness.** I was deeply affected by the negativity around me. I blindly went along with deadlines and schedules. I never asked to see the ledgers that were submitted to head office. I got stuck in trying to convert the negativity. Instead of following my inner guide, I just re-acted to opinions and outside circumstances.

WHY DO WE FOLLOW THE CROWD IN THE FIRST PLACE?

One reason sound decision-making is absent in many people's lives is that it is not taught in our educational system. To compound the challenge, not only is decision-making absent from the curriculum of our educational institutions, it's also lacking from most corporate training and human resource programs.

My father had a twenty-five-year career in corporate America. He was a department manager who really cared about his company. One day he decided to 'look into' the books of his department, which resulted in him challenging the record keeping. His boss appeared to be *cooking the books*. You might wonder if he was rewarded for having concern beyond his position. He was sacked immediately.

You see, most institutions do not want you asking questions or making intuitive decisions. That's why they tell you when to show up, what to wear, how much you will earn, where to stand or sit, what time to go for lunch, and when you will go on vacation. They also tell how often you need to come in on weekends or take work home with you. In Japan, it results in something called Karōshi (death from stress). In companies around the globe, that same stress results in depression, disease, and dissatisfaction. Corporations function, and even profit, but at what cost to their people? Individuals suffer simply because they are afraid to make a decision that could change the trajectory of their life.

"The fear of making a decision is the result of fearing to make a mistake - the truth is the fear of mistakes has a greater impact on you than making the mistake."

- Bob Proctor

So, you may be asking, "How do I develop the mental ability to make decisions and lose the fear of making a mistake?"

Follow the Guide Within

Dr. Abraham Maslow, who devoted his entire life to studying self-actualized people, stated that in order to become self-actualized, we must follow our inner guide and not be swayed by the opinions of others or by outside circumstances. His research showed that self-actualized decision makers have a number of things in common. They did work they felt was worthwhile and important, they found work a pleasure, and they had little distinction between work and play. Maslow also said that, not only do they do work they consider to be important and enjoyable, they do it well.

If you look at how most successful, self-actualized individuals spend the first two hours of their day, you will notice that they have specific habits that they have found to be important for success and life-long happiness. I recently asked Bob how he spends the first few hours of a typical day. Here is what he said:

5 - 5:10AM Rises

- Walks from his house, in his pajamas, along a pathway (heated in winter) by the swimming pool, to the backyard where his studio is located. *

- Opens his favorite book - *Think And Grow Rich* - and reads a section of it *ten* times.

- Reviews his schedule for the day.

- Returns to the house, showers, gets dressed (Bob is always dressed impeccably) and then enjoys breakfast with his wife, Linda.

- Goes back to the studio to start working. He stays busy, there is no wasted time. He said he loves what he does and that it doesn't feel like work; it is his passion to share his knowledge.

The Bottom Line - Bob is at work at the same time, or well before, the time when most people start work. But it is those first few hours of the day that are different than most people's (the masses). (note: When Bob was younger ...in his 70's... he would go to the gym before breakfast.)

*Repetition will bring order to your mind, which will help your decision making, which will in turn begin to improve the results in every area of your life. Reading inspirational lessons will begin to change your thoughts, which will change the vibration of what you attract, and ultimately, change your life.

That is why people who decide to leave the Mass mentality must learn to rely on the Law of Attraction. The second thing they must do is start making decisions.

*"You have to decide what you are going to do with your life!
Or you let the paradigm control you and march along in
lockstep-type fashion."*

- Bob Proctor

Making Decisions Brings Order to Your Life

The first and most important component of decision-making is speed. Making decisions must be done in a timely fashion. Ultimately, what drives business success is the quality of the decision and the timing of its implementation. Good decisions mean good business. Indecision is a choice in and of itself — a choice to take no action.

The ability to make the right decisions in a timely fashion is what defines you as an entrepreneur. It's NOT a skill that anyone was born with; it is a skill you learn as you improve your habits.

For new entrepreneurs, I recommend that you seek the assistance of a mentor you trust; do not be afraid to ask for advice from your peers and senior advisors. Remember, this is something you will eventually pay forward. When you succeed, you will be asked to mentor someone just as you are now asking someone to mentor you. Having a good mentor/guide is essential to avoiding the pitfalls inherent in business and in life. You can virtually eliminate conflict and confusion in every area of your life by becoming proficient at making decisions and by having a strong sounding board (your mentor).

"Indecision causes disintegration."

- Bob Proctor

How often have you heard a person say, "I don't know what to do?" And how often have you heard yourself say, "What should I do?" Think about some of the indecisive feelings you, and virtually everyone on this planet, experience from time to time. **Now** is the only time to take a serious look at your indecisiveness. Is there something in your life that you've been putting off? How about that New Year's Resolution that you made? Perhaps you keep saying that you're going to get a jump-start on your latest business idea — as soon as you have more time. Or perhaps it's more basic: putting off cleaning the house or washing the car. Even if you're putting off something that seems like a *minor thing,* don't kid yourself — it's not the size of what you're procrastinating about that's the problem. It's that you're giving energy to a bad habit that will grow and eventually strangle your success. A seemingly 'small' indecision grows and morphs into all forms of creative avoidance, which will haunt you the rest of your life.

So why do we hesitate?

Decisions can prove to be the hardest to make when it's a choice between where you think you **should** be and where you really **want** to be because that's the wrong question. The real question is, 'Are you ready to commit 100% to achieve the goal?' If the answer is *yes,* then the only thing left is to take action!

Decisions can be Magic

William Murray, a Scottish Himalayan Mountain climber, said it better than anyone. "Until one is committed there is hesitancy, the chance to draw back, always ineffectiveness. Concerning all acts of initiative and creation, there is one elementary truth, the ignorance of which kills countless ideas and splendid plans: that **the moment one definitely commits oneself, then Providence moves too**. All sorts of things occur to help one that would never otherwise have occurred. A whole stream of events issue from the decision, raising in one's favor all manner of unforeseen incidents and meetings and material assistance, which no man or woman could have dreamt would have come their way. So whatever you do, or dream you can do, begin it; boldness has genius and power and magic in it."

Most of the people I counsel don't want to commit to making a tough decision, even knowing that they will almost certainly face negative consequences because of their indecisiveness. Yet decisions (or the lack of them) are responsible for making or breaking a person's career; they can also impact relationships and health.

One of the reasons for indecisiveness is that decisions most often go against mass mentality. And most people you encounter and corporations you deal with, want you to stay in mass mentality. Leaving the Mass Consciousness is by definition an unpopular idea. Most people (*the **mass***) will think you have lost your mind. And hopefully you have lost your **mass** mind. As you take action, you might find that others see the change in you even before you see it in yourself. They might not embrace the change. As you read these words, take a mental inventory of all the relationships around you that involve mental manipulation; relationships that are keeping you stuck in *mass* mentality.

For over a half of a century my mentor has been creating his own path by simply committing. For the past two decades, I have watched him, time after time, make something incredible out of what seemed to be nothing. Like observing an individual crossing a bridge that only appears as they take the first step. That first step is called making a commitment.

"Leap, and the net will appear."

- John Burroughs

One of the first questions Bob asks someone he is coaching is, "What's the most money you have ever earned in a year and what year was that?" When I asked him why he always asks this question, he said, "Their answer is an indication of their decision-making ability, their level of awareness, and their current results. It is a picture of what they think they are capable of earning and just how aware they are at that moment."

Bob's question is an important question because of the very basic law of the universe, "create or disintegrate". Indecision causes disintegration.

Truth be told; the health of our mind and body, the well-being of our family, our social life, and the type of relationships we develop all are dependent upon our ability to make sound and decisive decisions and then our commitment to those decisions.

Making a decision is a vital step if you wish to enter the next level of Awareness, which is called **Aspiration**.

MENTOR'S MESSAGE

In this chapter on the **Second Level of Awareness,** we discussed the importance of making a decision. It is the only way to move away from Mass Consciousness to the next Level of Awareness. Most individuals either don't think about decisions or they get stuck in analysis paralysis.

Analysis paralysis is the state of over-analyzing (or over-thinking) a situation until a decision is never taken. In effect, paralyzing the outcome! A characteristic of good decision-making is that objectives are established; then classified and placed in order of importance. There are steps that are generally followed, which result in a 'decision model' that can be used to determine an optimal production plan. Movement, however small and in whatever direction, is preferable to doing nothing. At the very least, you'll find out what's not working or what you don't like and you can use that information to move in a different direction.

"Once you make a DECISION, the universe conspires to make it happen."

- Ralph Waldo Emerson

DECISION-MAKING TEMPLATE

I, _____ am so happy and grateful now that I have made a decision to act decisively on my future.

My decision is to _____.

It is so! I now charge this decision with enthusiasm.

Signed _____   Dated _____

The list of things that will need to be decided and acted on to fulfill my vision are:

1.

   _____
2.

   _____
3.

   _____
4.

   _____
5.

   _____
6.

   _____
7.

   _____
8.

   _____

WHAT TO DO / WHAT NOT TO DO

1. What do you most worry about? Be specific. Do you spend most of your thoughts worrying about the economy or thinking about what someone thinks about you? Since your thoughts ultimately control every decision you will make, what is one thought process you can change right now?

    _____

    _____

    _____

2. Do you follow the crowd rather than doing your own thinking or goal setting? Be honest.

    _____

    _____

    _____

3. Can you make a decision right now that, regardless of what happens today, you are going to look for the positive aspect of what's happening around you? If the answer is *yes*, go back to the Decision-Making Template and complete it. If the answer is *no*, why is that?

    _____

    _____

    _____

WORDS OF WISDOM

- All progress begins with a brave decision.

- The most important decision you can make is to be in a good mood.

- Successful people decide to make their dreams happen.

- Personal power is moved into action by decision.

- Create an Affirmation. I started with: "I have strong decision-making muscles."

- The more you love your decisions, the less you need others to love them.

- Find something to live for and die doing it.

You've got a whole series of decisions you could make today. Maybe you should stay right where you are, right this moment, and write out all the things that you have to make decisions on and make them one after another.

CHAPTER THREE

The 3rd Level of Awareness is called — Aspiration

You become aware of something inside you that wants more expression, wants a richer and fuller life. When that Aspiration becomes strong enough you will want to move away from the Masses. You will still be surrounded by the influences of the Masses and their thought processes but you won't be swayed by them. Always keep your encouraging thoughts and positive statements of Aspiration on your mind. Don't let the masses pull you back.

9:00 a.m. GST Copenhagen International Airport, Copenhagen, Denmark

It was July 6th, 2004, the day after Bob's seventieth birthday. We had spent his special day with an alchemist in the deep woods in the south of Sweden, and were now on a flight to Helsinki, Finland for a seminar. Bob was reading a Thomas Troward book that Gina Hayden, his Executive Assistant, had gifted him for his birthday. The book was a rare first edition titled *The Hidden Power*.

I was in seat 2D and Bob was seated right behind. He was starting to nod off so I asked him if I could take a look at the book. He jokingly said, "Don't spill anything on it William, it's a first edition."

Sometime during the flight, I started to nod off as well so I put the book in the seatback pocket for safe keeping. It wasn't until we were in the taxi that I realized I had left the book on the plane. I will never forget the sickening feeling that rushed to and through me. A bunch of questions flashed on the screen of my mind: "What should I say? When should I say it? Should I tell the truth or come up with some fantastic story to soften the blow?" I couldn't even imagine what Gina was going to say about my lack of responsibility; about how I had completely disregarded the time and money she had invested in acquiring this special gift for her long-time mentor. Later, at the hotel I blurted out the admission; I was nearly in tears. Bob looked at me and said, "Don't worry about it."

Now, I know Bob well enough to know that's not how he really felt. But he remained calm as he continued, "It wasn't meant to be. If it is meant to be, it will find its way back to me."

The title of the book was "The Hidden Power" by Thomas Troward. William was in for a huge lesson. If you ASK...BELIEVE AND EXPECT The Hidden Power will always deliver right on schedule... B

I kept thinking, "How? Your name and phone number weren't in it? What else could possibly go wrong?"

When the taxi pulled up to our hotel we realized that the event coordinator in Finland had booked us into a YMCA. There were two tiny rooms with an army cot in each. A TV was above the door because there was no other location for it. My suitcase wouldn't fit in the room unless I put it under the cot and my six-foot-six-inch body wouldn't fit in the bathroom. I only knew that somehow I had to shower and get ready for the busy day ahead. As I was trying to shave, with one leg outside the bathroom and one inside, Bob knocked on the door and said, "Stay in your room, I'll be right back." Forty minutes later he was back. "Pack your bags. We're out of here," was all he said. He had found a five-star hotel; my room had a bathroom that ten people could fit into. The hotel problem was solved but I continued to feel awful and ashamed about losing the book.

"Always remember, believing is seeing,
not the other way around."

-Bob Proctor

During our stay in Helsinki, I spent what seemed like hours on hold with the airline's Lost & Found Department in Germany praying with everything I had in me that Bob's book would show up. My phone bill ended up being more expensive than the hotel room! I finally managed to talk with an English-speaking customer-service representative who told me that our plane had gone on to Latvia, then back to Germany and was now in Spain. Oh boy!

When we flew out of Helsinki a couple days later, I thought I would make one more attempt to find the book. I left Bob at the gate and ran down to the baggage claim area. There was no one there, only a sign on the door that read, "We will return in one hour." There was a courtesy phone for after-hour claims, so I picked it up and a man answered and said, "How may I help you?"

His perfect English caught me off guard because I thought I would be talking to someone using my broken German again. So I just said, "Yeah ... I was just inquiring about a book that was left on a plane two days ago. It's a Thomas Troward, first edition, leather bound, antique-looking book, and it's brown." To which he replied, "Hold on." And a few minutes later as the top half of the Lost & Found door sprang open, the man said, "Is this the book you are looking for?" By the time I got back to the gate, the plane was already boarding. Bob said, "Where were you? Have you been in the bathroom this whole time?" I said jokingly, "No. I had a hunch there might be a bookstore in the airport with a First Edition Troward" and handed him his book. He grinned and said, "You are just about the luckiest son of a gun I've ever met." All I felt was relief.

Bob always shows me what he teaches me. He had told me the Universe delivers on the level of your ability to believe (even when the odds are stacked against you and even when there is no name or forwarding address tucked in a priceless book). Like he said, "If it is meant to be, it will find its way back to me."

So Here's the Question:

When we know that life can be better, why don't we then take responsibility for making it better?

There are many reasons why individuals don't take responsibility. Perhaps you were told that you were ordinary and that you should just be grateful for what you have. While gratitude for what you have is a prerequisite for hooking up with what Bob calls the Architect of the Universe, it must also be applied to the rest of what you have been given. Perhaps, at a weak moment, you found it easier to let others take responsibility for your life. That decision became a habit and others (often well-meaning individuals) gradually took over your power. The more you relinquished your power, the less you created, and the further you sank back into mass mentality.

Yet you are a creator and you have access to the laws which are designed to help you create whatever you determine to accomplish. It starts with gratitude but it will go nowhere without attitude, action, and aspiration.

> *"The image of your goal properly planted and constantly nourished with positive, expectant thought-energy will cause your goal to develop into a burning desire."*
>
> *- Bob Proctor*

Desire Without Action

Responsibility is a choice. I had never learned the benefits or disadvantages that were associated with this very powerful phrase so there wasn't any possibility of me comprehending what Bob meant when he talked about the freedom that responsibility could offer in one's life journey.

I think it would be fair to say that the people for whom we have the greatest respect for have accepted responsibility in every aspect of their lives. These individuals don't duck responsibility by blaming someone else. When faced with an unfavorable situation, they are usually aware that they attracted the negative circumstance. When they err, they merely learn their lesson. They don't quit or abandon the goal, they just keep reaching for the new frontier. They have learned to take responsibility for whatever happens, every step of the way. Failure is not an enemy. It is just a lesson.

I mentor people to take responsibility so their future can be everything they have ever dreamed and then some. As Bob says, "You have the talent and tools to experience one beautiful day after another. It is what I have come to believe the Architect of the Universe had in mind for us when we were created. If that was not so, we would have never been endowed with such incredible faculties."

But accepting the status quo can create a kind of 'soul apathy'. We stop dreaming and hoping because we have accepted circumstances and outside events to be our destiny rather than taking responsibility for the outcome of our lives. Yet we were created to aspire and so, in order to lead a better, richer, more fulfilling and more balanced life, we must aspire to create.

Here, Take my Keys

I strongly believe that there are Five Key elements needed for a balanced, successful life. I have also learned that I need to check them regularly — much as I would check my blood pressure or my bank account. They are key performance indicators in the business world and critical philosophical pillars in the spiritual aspects of life; I have come to see them as the keys to having abounding happiness and optimum health.

The Five Keys are:

- Mind
- Body
- Family
- Community
- Finances

I have been using and evaluating these Five Keys for over two decades. Bob taught me how to improve my **Mind** with positive thought and focused action. I was fortunate to get an understanding of complementary medicine and exercise to help keep me **Physically Healthy**. I met and married my Australian dream girl and she has helped me to be better in and around my **Family**. And my love for mentoring and teaching has given me a super passion for helping my **Community** and my world.

However, I have never understood or focused much on my monetary outcomes. My **Financial** results have been all over the place. I had very good years and other years when I would barely squeak by. But what was the cause of those financial roller-coaster highs and lows? I was clear on the effects and the feelings and emotions that came from both sides of the outcome, but why the vicissitudes — big highs and near bankruptcy lows? In a word: It was my paradigm and it all came down to three big factors:

1. My attitude towards money

2. My poor decision-making ability concerning money

3. My refusal to take responsibility with respect to money

Simply stated, I would find it easier to blame everyone and everything for my failures in both my personal and professional life. I continued to reject my individuality and always turned all of my special powers over to other people, situations, or circumstances. When I operated according to my faulty paradigm, I was no longer in control of my future. It was a bit sad really. I was constantly hoping something good would happen, but given my thinking (paradigm) I would habitually attract something I did not want to happen. So let me be clear: It requires great courage to take responsibility for your life. It seems much easier to blame someone else or something outside of you.

"People are always blaming their circumstances for what they are. I don't believe in circumstances. The people who get on in this world are the people who get up and look for the circumstances they want, and, if they can't find them, they make them."

-- George Bernard Shaw

CHANGE YOUR THOUGHTS

I believe George Bernard Shaw was right. Most people believe that people and circumstances are responsible for the outcome of their lives. Yet in order to move through and past the Aspiration Level, it is crucial to take responsibility for all aspects of your life beginning with your thoughts.

In my mentor's opinion, those who win big in life take responsibility and create their own destiny. So when it comes to finances (and just about every other facet of your life) there is one big factor that will determine your results. Curious? Okay, here it is: There is a vast difference between being responsible for and being responsible to. It may be a blinding flash of the obvious, but don't let the simplicity fool you. I'm going to repeat it again. There is a BIG difference between being responsible FOR and being responsible TO.

> *"You may believe that you are responsible for what you do, but not for what you think. The truth is that you are responsible for what you think, because it is only at this level that you can exercise choice. What you do comes from what you think."*

> *- Marianne Williamson*

It's not uncommon these days to hear a parent blame themselves and assume responsibility for something that happened to their child, and that 'child' might be forty years old! "If we only..." Or, "I should have ..." We can all fill in the blanks, right? Their parental responsibility ended years ago and yet they still think they are responsible for their 'child' and they are still bailing their 'child' out. Now before the good parents of America come and get me, let me say that there is a time when this is not true. You are responsible both TO and FOR raising children up to the age of maturity.

My generation has been called the 'Sandwich' generation because we are responsible for those who came before us (parents) and those who came after us (kids). Add to the list: down-on-their-luck siblings, can't-get-it-together staff members... no wonder mid-lifers are feeling stressed.

I had to be reminded of the difference between support and enabling; the difference between being cold-hearted and letting go with love.

This is just one more excellent reason to have a close relationship with a Mentor. Bob has had to remind me on numerous occasions about the difference between a hand-up and a hand-out. Bottom line: good judgement requires objectivity — often difficult when dealing with people we love and care about.

So here is your 'wake-up call'.

CHANGE YOUR ATTITUDE

The proper way to look at this is that you are responsible FOR your feelings and your results, but not for other people's feelings and results. You may be responsible TO another person for one thing or another, but you are not responsible FOR another person.

And if we look at the situation of me forgetting Bob's birthday gift on the plane: I was both responsible TO and FOR the safe return of his book. But I was never responsible for how Bob reacted or felt about it. This is an important difference. The old William would have attempted to make up some lame excuse or blame it on some fictitious thief. Yes, it's true!

The old William would have tried to put the blame on another person or the airline and then trick myself into believing that I would then be free to play, free to have fun. By not taking responsibility, I could then manipulate how Bob felt about me and what had happened.

It would not enter my mind that exactly the opposite would happen.

When I don't take responsibility for something, I permit (or force) others to take on my responsibilities — and I become dependent on them. Our roles reverse: they become the giver and I become the receiver. My well-being then becomes dependent upon their generosity. At some point during my mentoring with Bob, it became very clear that this kind of behavior only leads to a life of lack, limitation, resentment, and confusion on the parts of both the giver and the receiver.

"Responsibility is the price of greatness."

- Winston Churchill

CHANGE YOUR BEHAVIOR

Challenge the Status Quo

I've never witnessed anything positive that has come from the misuse of responsibility. When you take on the responsibility for another person's feelings, results, or actions, you destroy their self-reliance and self-respect. Those who haven't taken responsibility for their results and their life often find themselves in a mental prison and a cycle of blame/shame closely followed by anger and apathy (depression). Mental prisons can destroy just about everything that is necessary for a meaningful life: purpose, fulfilment, self-respect, relationships, and physical health.

"My philosophy is that not only are you responsible for your life, but doing the best at this moment puts you in the best place for the next moment."

- Oprah Winfrey

Responsibility and the Flying Nun

Immediately following the lost book episode in Helsinki, we boarded a flight to Frankfurt. The concourses are enormous in Frankfurt; we had already walked a long way to get to our gate and our connecting flight to London was about to board. We were just a few gates away when an elderly Catholic Nun (who barely reached the bottom of Bob's tie) approached Bob and stood right in front of him. Out of all the thousands of people in the airport she picked Bob (who is neither Catholic or particularly approachable when he is focused on catching a flight). She was obviously distraught and started talking quickly and loudly in Italian, all the while waving her boarding pass in the air. Neither of us speak Italian so I was surprised to see Bob put his hand gently on her shoulder as he reached down and looked at the boarding pass. She was headed to Rome so we walked with her to the Arrival & Departure Board to find her gate and then point her in the right direction.

She obviously didn't understand because she continued to talk even more quickly and loudly. Bob suddenly put her arm under his, told me to take her suitcase (which was one of those old cloth-covered hard cases from days gone by) and all three of us walked her to her gate at the opposite end of the concourse — at least twenty minutes away. When we arrived, Bob walked up to the airline agent and said, "Look, I need you to take care of this Holy Sister. Make sure she's escorted onto the plane. Make sure she gets into her seat. She has been lost, and she's upset. Upon arrival in Rome, she should also be escorted to her destination." Bob then sat her down, put her suitcase next to her and made sure that she was okay. She smiled and blessed him with what can only be described as a spiritual outpouring. The experience was something I will never forget.

As we walked back to our gate, I turned to Bob and said, "That was interesting." He just smiled. I continued, "You know, out of the thousands of people in this concourse, she picked you. What do you think that's all about?" His response was typical Proctor. He said, "She understands vibrational energy, William. You see, she knew as well as I knew, without speaking the same language or having ever met before, that the Law of Attraction put both of us together at exactly the right time at the precise location. And as you worried about missing our flight, I just trusted the process and knew that a Higher Power was in control of the circumstance. I knew that even if the job of delivering her to the gate would cost us missing our flight, there would be an allowance for that because the world is in perfect order."

"And by the way," Bob quipped, "For my actions, I will be going to heaven but I am unsure about the rest of you who chose not to come to her ald."

When we finally reached our gate, we found out that there was a thirty-minute delay in boarding. Bob asked me as we sat down, "Would you like to know how to read an individual's vibration?" "Of course," I said, "Absolutely, I would."

> **Bob's Handwritten Coaching Comment**
>
> ⊗The lesson with the flying NUN was a good one for William. When you wonder what you should do, follow the quiet voice within. It is always perfect... 🅑

I'm Picking-up Good Vibrations

As Bob explained, I was reminded of when I first showed him a photo of Deborah and he said, "She's left brain and right brain. She would make a great attorney, or an accountant, or a cop." Unbeknownst to Bob, Deborah had been a fifteen-year veteran of the Victoria Police force in Melbourne, Australia. But just as with the Catholic Nun, it was like he was able to understand Deborah, read her energy, and connect with who she is, if only by a photo. As we sat, he said, "Look at this guy coming here... let me tell you about him... and let me tell you about that gal over there... and let me tell you about this individual coming to your right." He said it was simple, "Whatever's going on, on the outside of an individual is a reflection of what's going on, on the inside of them. Got it?"

So simple I almost missed it.

MENTOR'S MESSAGE

In this chapter on the *Level of Aspiration,* I discussed the importance of taking responsibility for the outcome of every aspect of life.

In 2002, I saved myself from the brink of utter failure in all aspects of my life, including near financial collapse simply by taking responsibility!

Back then, I was at a very low point in my life where I felt like it just couldn't get any worse – surley! I could see no way out of the hole I had dug myself. All the blame and lack of responsibility I had been verbalizing had reached a tipping point. I was my own worst enemy. The reason I was getting poor results in my life was not because of bad luck or lousy circumstances. It was because I was blocking all the good by continuing to blame and complain.

Yet each moment, each situation, each turn of events presents us with an opportunity to accept responsibility for building the self we are capable of being. It is not about complaining and blaming. It is about accepting opportunities, implementing ideas, taking action, and actively expressing the purpose that is uniquely ours.

Ultimately it is about taking responsibility.

WHAT TO DO/WHAT NOT TO DO

1. Examine your life today and the results you are getting. Are you still playing the victim, using self-justification, or excusing yourself by blaming others, or are you now willing to accept responsibility for your actions? If so, find and keep people in your life who will help keep you accountable.

    _____

    _____

    _____

2. What is something that you really want/aspire to achieve in life? Write it down (in the present tense – as if you have already achieved it). Do you feel worthy to have the goal that you desire? If not, why not?

    _____

    _____

    _____

3. Remember the story about how Bob can determine what a person is about just by what's going on, on the outside of them? What does your outside YOU say about you? What is one thing you can you do to change the outside?

    _____

    _____

    _____

WORDS OF WISDOM

- You are responsible for your own behavior.

- Other's nonsense does not have to change your mood, your decisions, or your behavior.

- Taking responsibility allows you to make better decisions.

- You are the mental architect of your own destiny.

- It's YOUR responsibility to make the necessary changes to achieve the results YOU desire.

- You've got to take personal responsibility to make it happen and you've got to resolve within yourself, that "You can do this."

You are responsible for all of the results in your life. You are responsible for your happiness. You are responsible for your health. You are responsible for your wealth. And you are responsible for your emotional state. Regardless of what has happened in the past, the future lies ahead with an open slate, waiting for you to take control and create a wonderful life for yourself.

CHAPTER FOUR

Individual

The 4th Level of Awareness is – Individual

The Individual Consciousness Level is when you begin to express your uniqueness as a human being. From this point on, forget about what everyone else is doing. Forget about what kind of person you think they want you to be and just be the most authentic version of the person you are. Think of personal development as the act of upgrading every area of your life — health, finances, relationships... to function at the highest possible level. Virtually all aspects of personal development lead to greater conscious development in one way or another. Let who you are as an Individual and what you believe in shine through in every word you speak and every move you make.

8:30 a.m. EST Florida Turnpike West Palm Beach, FL

It was an absolutely beautiful morning on September 11th, 2001. I had just made one of the biggest decisions in my entrepreneurial career. It was going to take focus and commitment but I was ready. Not only had less than fifty individuals realized the rank in my company I had set my sites on, but I was going to be one of the youngest to reach this pinnacle. It was a big step that would raise my income by millions of dollars. As I drove north on the Florida turnpike, I was excited to be meeting with the last cog in the wheel and his team at Einstein Bagels just off Indiantown Road in Jupiter, Florida. It was a 10:00 am meet up and I was on time; a bit early as I always had the belief that being on time demonstrated my hard-earned responsible attitude.

My rental car was filled with the sounds of a positive mental attitude recording when I noticed an unusual number of people pulling off to the side of the road. They were all getting out of their cars and consoling each other. What was going on? I turned on my radio because this was obviously not a typical 'car breakdown' situation. The radio was tuned into the Howard Stern show live from New York. Stern was reporting that a jetliner had just crashed into one of the World Trade Center towers. As I was listening in disbelief, he said, "Oh my God, here comes another one!" The impact that followed was unfathomable. Life as I understood it, from that second forward, would never be the same. It wouldn't be the same for anyone.

As I walked into my meeting, the laughter and smiles emanating from my business associates was familiar and strangely comforting. It all felt surreal. I was there as the one guy who could bring their goals and dreams to reality but they were still unaware of what was taking place just a few hours north up the eastern seaboard.

As I told them of the tragic situation, a team member broke into tears and ran out of the cafe. We later learned that his brother was in one of the towers, an employee of the investment firm, Cantor Fitzgerald. As we disbanded, I will never forget the look on the face of my key player. He said, "What does all of this mean with regards to our business plan over the next ninety days?" I said, "There will be no business conducted over the next ninety days and I'm not so sure we will be back to business in the following ninety days either." It was something none us had ever even considered. I remember how quiet the trip back to Ft. Lauderdale was. Mobile phones were down, there was no traffic on the turnpike, and even the chatter on the radio had turned to shock and silence; words could not describe the reality of the terror attack that had just taken place.

Bob's Handwritten Coaching Comment

I said "William if you are not prepared to face the thing you fear and go where you have never been. You will always stay where you are..."

"There is no problem outside of you that is superior to the power within you."

- Bob Proctor

The Terror Barrier

That horrible day, 9/11, influenced heads of government, corporate leaders, and individuals (both in our nation and around the globe) to rethink their priorities. I decided that rather than let the terror derail me, I would begin a whole new attitude.

Looking back, the Terror Barrier had reared its ugly head every time I attempted to make a major move in my life. Whenever I ventured into an area I had never traveled before, I let the accumulated inheritance of others' habits, opinions, and belief systems (paradigms) control me. The paradigms had so much power and strength that at the slightest hint of fear or weakness, they would take over and I would regress. As the paradigms of not being good enough or not smart enough took control, I would slide back down the ladder to where it all began — into the Animalistic behavior of fight, freeze, or flee. It happened as naturally as sun rise and it seemed fundamental to my development (or lack thereof).

"Paradigms don't originate with you. They're the accumulated inheritance of other people's habits, opinions, and belief systems. Yet they remain the guiding force in YOUR life. There will be no permanent change in your life until the paradigm has been changed."

- Bob Proctor

Whenever I thought that I'd made the break for freedom, I found the old Terror Barrier rearing up in front of me. Now, couple that with a terrorist attack of biblical proportions and you might agree that I had what seemed to be an impossible task regarding my personal work goal and desire. But I had spent the previous decade listening to inspirational tapes and doing daily repetitions of motivational readings and all those tapes and books and readings had instilled in me the belief that I shouldn't let any Terror Barrier (or Terror Attack) turn me from my greatest dreams.

The Terror Barrier is just that imaginary wall that stands between where we are and where we've never been, but want to go. Our greatest triumphs lie just beyond our greatest fear — and there's only one way to get to the other side — change our paradigm. I eventually regained my calm and began witnessing the world come together against this hideous act of weakness. I was lifted up and given an intuitive thought. I wasn't to abandon my dreams and desires; I was to simply change the date.

To overcome my terror barriers, I had to remain aware enough to focus on what lies on the other side of that terror barrier. It is courage that is required to see beyond the event; to live in the solution not the problem, to have faith.

The old date was not important. What mattered to me, and to a great many other people, was that I hit my goal — in the face of terror — that WE hit our goal.

I made a commitment that before September 30, 2002 I would reach the goal that I had set on September 11, 2001. I knew deep within, that I would not blame a terror attack or anyone or anything else for my lack of success. That new resolve made all things possible. I reached my goal exactly one year later!

> *"Just keep marching, no matter how badly your feet want to stay rooted to the ground. Refuse to permit this negative demon to control you; your emotions; your future."*
>
> *- William Todd*

What is It That You Most Desire and What is Your Fear Around that Desire?

It's predictable that we will run into a wall of fear when we go after our dreams. Well, at least most of us do. Because there is a part of the mind that loves negative chatter like, "You can't do that," or "You aren't smart enough."

But by using repetition of positive mantras, we can create enough positive consciousness around what we desire that it will drown out the old paradigms of doom and gloom.

Bob says there are two ways to change a paradigm:

1. Constant spaced repetition of ideas that are essentially opposite to the paradigm.

2. Personal experience after an emotional impact. *

*An emotional impact is usually a life-changing experience – a life-threatening disease, divorce, or the death of someone close to us.

Some individuals make life-changing shifts after experiencing a life-changing experience — not always, but sometimes. Most of us need to reprogram our paradigms with repetition of thought followed by action. This is Individual growth; it is the key to a healthy and successful life because what we think about (our paradigm) ultimately manifests in our life.

> *"You and your results are the product of someone else's habitual way of thinking."*
>
> *- Bob Proctor*

I've Succeeded! Now What?

When my 2002 goal had been reached, my personal life stabilized, and my business was booming, I began to think that I had arrived. I was grateful as I remembered that continuing education and repetitious learning had been such an important part of my journey; but I also started to think that it was something that I didn't need to be as disciplined with anymore. Big Mistake!

It became apparent to me, after much fanfare and celebration, that without another written goal, I was headed for some of the same results that I had just overcome. I asked Bob if it was possible for me to fall back into my old habits? He just stared at me and said frankly that the development of individuality is a never-ending process. The choices we make, the aspirations we develop, the use of our talents and capacities — all are paramount to being a fully individualized human being.

Amazing, really. I had seen it happen to countless other people I had mentored and here I was doing the same thing. I had foolishly turned a blind-eye to the unbelievable force that is constantly pulling and tugging away at our belief systems and mindset; like a gravitational pull that is constantly attempting to draw us back into our old habits. I describe it as watching a magnet in a junk yard pick up an automobile and lift it to great heights, only to drop it into a bin and crush it to a fraction of its original size.

Certainly, I was excited to be a witness to *The Mentor in Me* being un-earthed; I appreciated the gift that the good Lord granted me in being able to be a coach and watch so many unfoldings and breakthroughs but it was time for me to get back on track. I have a friend who says, "Never turn your back on the ocean." I had turned my back on the ocean and the tide was about to pull me in. It was time to win back my self-esteem by doing esteem-able things.

Find Something You Would Die for and Live for It

In Mid-August of 2004, while driving from Sedona, Arizona to Colorado, we made a stopover at a unique five-star ranch on the Colorado River in Moab, Utah called Sorrell River Ranch. At breakfast the next morning I told Deborah that this would be an excellent location for a leadership event. After reaching a level of success, I had been overcome with a vision. That vision was to share what my mentor and coach was doing for me; to teach others about the **Seven Levels of Awareness**. I remember calling Bob and telling him about my goal and he said, "How close is the nearest international airport?" I told him Denver, Colorado or Salt Lake City, Utah which were each just over five hours away. He said, "Go for it!"

The ranch event was a serious stretch. I was out of my comfort zone but I was back in development.

We leave our comfort zone because we realize that this departure is necessary for change to take place. All growth takes place outside our comfort zone. When we take strong enough actions, and harness our desire, our old paradigms become void — they are obscured in a flurry of activity that allows our desire to overtake those old habits, which is how we eventually develop a tacit understanding of individualism.

It Takes Courage to be an Individual

The next time you are encouraged to fall into line, to be a sport and say yes while everything inside of you is saying no, be courageous and say NO. There is no meaningful compensation for conformity.

This project was a big undertaking but on my forty-third birthday in the first week of October, my vision from August the year before was realized in Moab, Utah at the Sorrell River Ranch Resort. I hosted the first ever "Lead the Field" Leadership Event with Bob Proctor. It was a sellout event. This vision, this crazy idea of putting together a leadership session with top business leaders from all over the world at a place called the Sorrel River Ranch, which is five hours away from any International airport was attended by people from Norway, Germany, Israel, Australia, Canada, and Latin America.

It was an incredible event in a breathtaking setting. Bob likes to surprise people with presenting them with thoughtful gifts. He owned an unpublished document from a prominent foundation, one that no one had ever seen. He had it printed and placed into beautiful leather-bound binders. His plan was to pack the binders into substantial-looking black boxes that were to be wrapped with enormous red bows. A wonderful surprise for all who attended. The challenge was the last-minute arrival of the boxes. But since we were now totally convinced that this was a great idea we decided that we would get them prepared regardless of time. And so, at 5:30 am before the first session, the staff was frantically boxing up the binders and wrapping the red ribbon and big bows on each one. The event was outdoors in an amphitheater and it was still dark. In that early morning and out of that darkness emerged Bob and Linda in their pajamas and slippers to help us place these beautiful gifts onto white linen-draped tables for that amazing crowd. Even my vivid imagination couldn't have come up with this powerful picture of what we had created. The sunrise shining on the red rock mesa's landscape illuminating the beautiful white tables stacked with black boxes, adorned with red ribbon. All I could think was, "This guy just... he just never stops giving."

Even a Top Mentor gets Stretched

During the retreat, we all had a choice of extra-curricular activities. There was horseback riding, white-water rafting, or quad runners. Bob and Linda, Deborah and I decided to go horseback riding with a group of attendees. Bob got a horse called *Big John;* it was no misnomer. It was for real, Bob practically did the splits to straddle this giant animal. After three-and-a-half hours of riding he could barely walk. Someone went into town and got Epsom salts for him so he could soak until he was able to stand and teach later that night. I reflected that Bob, at 71 years of age, not only emceed a major event but also went on a three-hour horseback ride. Few seventy-plus-year old individuals could or would do that but Bob always leads by example and he definitely knows when to work and when to play.

As we were setting up for the evening session, Bob suddenly headed towards the main lodge. When I asked him where he was going, he said he had just heard that one of the participants had broken his leg on the quad; that he was in a lot of pain. He was going to be taken into Phoenix the next morning but Bob wanted to hypnotize him so he could sleep through the night and make the trip without any pain. I said, "What?" I couldn't believe my ears. "Yeah," Bob said, "You've never seen me do that?" And then he invited Deborah and us to watch. As Bob stood next to this poor fellow's bed, he took a cheap hotel pen in hand and said, "Now, I'm going to hypnotize you. I'm going to transfer all the pain that you're experiencing from your leg into this pen. I want you to listen carefully and just know that at the end of this hypnosis this pen is going to assume all the pain that's in your leg." The procedure and the transformation took less than a half an hour. When I saw the guy the next morning as he was being readied for the trip to Phoenix, he was still gripping the pen! I was later told that he slept with it. His face showed no sign of pain or discomfort. I jokingly went up to him and said, "May I borrow your pen for a moment to write a note?" And he just looked at me with eyes that said, "Nobody is getting this pen!"

Other than the broken leg incident, the event was a great success on so many levels except... we discovered that we were way over our budget on food thanks to a manager who upped the price per head after the contract had been signed. Deborah and I were having a conversation with the property owner on how to resolve the bill when Bob came over. He could tell that we were upset. It wasn't like we could go back to over a hundred participants and say, "Hey, they upped the price on all the food." The fact was that we owed thousands of dollars more than we had agreed upon.

I was about to learn another lesson because Bob whipped out his black American Express card and said, "Don't worry about it. Here, put it on this card." It was a moment in time. It was lucid. He taught me so much about money: what it is, that you don't make it — you actually earn it; what you can do with it; that there's never been this much money in circulation in our history. And now this: It wasn't just about him taking responsibility and footing the bill for the extra food — it was how he showed me that I was still holding onto my old paradigms about money. I was raised with a lack of money mentality. My father would say, "Money doesn't grow on trees." If it did, my parents wouldn't have had to file for bankruptcy not once, but twice, and we wouldn't have been evicted from our home for non-payment. But instead of giving money power, in that moment Bob taught me to transform my relationship with money from one of scarcity and pain to one of sufficiency, abundance, and inspiration. Yes, he footed the bill for the extra charges but more importantly he helped me change my paradigm to one that said that money is good when we are good managers of it. It was so vivid and clear! This event was where I really began to believe in myself and to open up a positive pathway for my potential. It is where I started to become the true, unique, free, and creative version of William. Once I got out of my own way, trusted the process, stopped just hearing my old paradigms and started listening to my mentor's truths; then my ideas became plans, my possibilities became opportunities, and my potential became unlimited. Your potential is unlimited as well.

The entire Universe is controlled by the Law of CIRCULATION. You must keep everything moving. You never own anything. If you aren't let it go, it owns you...

"The success gene lives in every person regardless of the results they are presently getting - we are spiritual beings and spirit is always for expansion and fuller expression."

- Bob Proctor

CHANGE YOUR THOUGHTS

Do the One Thing You Fear

When faced with your Terror Barrier, you might break out in a cold sweat, find yourself covered in hives, or feel your heart palpitate even though you are nowhere near danger. You see, your perception IS your reality! You may not know exactly what lies on the other side of your Terror Barrier, but there's no question that once you get through the fear, you'll be much closer to your goal. And as Bob often says, "If your goal doesn't scare and excite you at the same time, you're going after the wrong goal."

I faced so many terror barriers hosting that leadership retreat. There were more than a few times when events didn't go exactly as planned and my thoughts threatened to derail me and the outcome. Fortunately, I had a mentor who had already visualized a successful outcome.

Here is a good exercise: Name your Terror Barrier. Then begin to visualize yourself successfully wrecking that Terror Barrier of yours. Mentally see yourself winning and you will start to liberate yourself from the crippling emotional state that the Terror Barrier caused.

Remember, perception IS reality!

CHANGE YOUR ATTITUDE

Trust Intuition and Take Action

There are many other benefits for you too. After aspiring to something bigger and better than your current circumstances, you can begin to acknowledge that you are a worthwhile, amazing individual who is capable of amazing things. You finally KNOW you are an Individual! This is when you begin to express your individuality as a human being. You become aware that there never has been, and there will never be, another expression of life like you. You are out of your head and into your individuality. Because there is no one like you. You move into action because you were created to achieve your goal. You have earned the awareness and the faith to move forward with your goals and desires. But you must do the work each day, one day at a time to stay in development.

Our mentors were right: *If you can think it, you can do it*. It is a powerful principle of human development. Keep your mind only on the things you desire. Refuse to live in a problem. Now you know why it was as simple as taking out my written goal and changing the year to 2002. I accept that I must work with the circumstances but I refuse to be ruled by circumstances. Just applying what I had listened to, hundreds of times, changed my life. I began to dream again.

We all need to remember that we are worthwhile individuals who are capable of amazing things. There is a marvelous inner-world that exists within you, and the revelation of such a world enables you to do; to attain; and to achieve your worthy desire. Only you possess your special gifts and talents.

> *"Know what is happening around you.*
> *Be in control of what is happening within you."*
> *- Bob Proctor*

CHANGE YOUR BEHAVIOR

Follow Through on Your Commitments

In his essay, "Self-Reliance" Ralph Waldo Emerson defines individualism as a profound and unshakeable trust in one's own intuitions. Reconnecting with the unbounded creativity seen in youth, according to Emerson, is one of the most powerful means for achieving inward self-reliance. As soon as I stepped back into the action, everything that I was seeking was also seeking me. I begin to live on purpose instead of by chance.

So, to begin to express your Individuality as a human being, you must take action. Remember that there has never been anyone like you before and never will be again. To hold these beliefs requires self-discipline. Bob says that self-discipline is giving yourself an order and then making yourself obey. Most of us don't have enough self-respect when we begin. There is so much talk about gaining self-esteem today, but in my experience the only way you will ever 'esteem' yourself is when you have learned to trust yourself.

We make commitments and don't make ourselves accountable to the fulfillment of those obligations, especially if it is something good for us. That has to change.

Please make a commitment to think about what you are asking yourself to do and then to do it! Do the right thing based in principle and not mass thinking or for other motives like money. All the accolades in the world will never compare to the feeling you gain by respecting yourself enough to follow your dreams and to follow through on your commitments.

Remember that you are a worthwhile individual who is capable of amazing things. There is a marvelous inner-world that exists within you, and the revelation of such a world enables you to do, to attain, and to achieve your worthy desire. Only you possess your special gifts and talents.

"The only limits in our life are those we impose on ourselves."
- Bob Proctor

MENTOR'S MESSAGE

Ralph Waldo Emerson defines individualism as a profound and unshakeable trust in one's own intuition. My wife Deborah has taught me the power of intuition. Being intuitive means that you are able to tap into an unlimited intelligence to receive guidance about your life's purpose. Intuition can be used to receive direction for your own life or for the guidance required to mentor other people. I remember so many occasions where Deborah said, "I don't have a good feeling about this place, that route, that individual, or this business deal." She was also gracious enough not to say, "I told you so," when I didn't listen. So why do we resist or even ignore intuition when it is such a large part of our awareness?

My most impactful example of intuition regarding Deborah's counsel was with a friend and business colleague. While he was a close friend, our daily conversations left me absolutely drained. Upon awakening each day my cell phone would already contain a voice-message with a lengthy message of mostly negative talk. I was so accustomed to these daily negative brainstorming sessions that I had actually began to think I was helping him by responding. But then there were always those polite cautions from Deborah, suggesting that I was completely and totally ignorant to what was taking place. I couldn't see the truth because it had gone on like that for several years. It had become a habit.

In his book, *Prosperity Through Thought Force* MacLellan states, "Sympathy bestowed on others is only wasted strength. They hold all that is given like a leech and crave the more, since it is being given, but it destroys their self-reliance and weakens the giver until, if persisted in, it would reduce one to mental poverty and leave the other high and dry on the shoals of dependence with no one strong enough to lean on for support." This quote was totally true for my relationship with this friend and Deborah's intuition was spot on, because the toll that it took on me and so many other members of his family, friends, and business associates was daunting. My last conversation with him was just a few days short of his birthday. I had asked him to please be careful with his anxiety and stress levels. I reminded him what impact his thoughts were having on his well-being. My lovely wife reminded me that I had been verbalizing this same warning for many months, if not years.

We learned of his passing from a massive heart attack just days later while we were poolside in Napa Valley California celebrating Deborah's birthday. Ironically, the Napa Valley was one of my friend's favorite places to visit. We were in shock and dismay. It was a major reality check and I finally had to admit that all my sympathy hadn't changed a thing. As I look back and as I look forward, I realize how vulnerable we are in negative brainstorming sessions and how important it is that we protect our spiritual space.

"Self-confidence is a must for a fulfilled life. If you have a divine self-confidence, you know how fortunate you are. Study yourself, you have awareness and infinite power within you. Choose to build an image in your marvelous mind of what you want to do. Happiness, health and prosperity will be your rewards."

- Bob Proctor

WHAT TO DO/WHAT NOT TO DO

1.   Setting goals takes time. Take a day to reflect — and then set a goal to achieve something that is so BIG, so exhilarating that it excites you and scares you at the same time. My goal and the time-frame is:

   _____

   _____

   _____

2.   Ask yourself: Where do I want to be one year from today? Your question (and answer) can be on any or all the Key Areas from Chapter Three –

   Mind/Body/Family/Community/Finances.

   _____

   _____

   _____

3.   Write out the following (change the words if they don't quite fit) affirmation:

   I am the artist of my reality. Every choice I make, every action I take, every thought I think contributes to my beautiful life.

   _____

   _____

   _____

WORDS OF WISDOM

- A strong sense of individualism and persistence are essential attributes of successful entrepreneurs.

- Believe in the power of thought and intention.

- Pursue whatever you wish to achieve in your world.

- Putting a great deal of willpower behind your actions will make you much more likely to succeed.

- You have been gifted with mental faculties to improve any circumstance around you.

- Don't be a victim of negative self-talk, remember you are listening.

- Change is inevitable but personal growth is a choice.

Figure out which people you genuinely like, instead of which ones you want to like you. Hang out with people you think are cool, instead of those you'd like to be considered cool by. Get to know people by telling your own true stories and listening to theirs. Do things because they interest you, not because you think they make you look interesting to others.

CHAPTER FIVE

Discipline

The 5th Level of Awareness is called —Discipline

Discipline is giving yourself a command and following it. This is how you distance yourself from the masses. This is how you demonstrate your individuality and distinctiveness. You move from Individual to Discipline by using Aspiration to empower your ideas and your individuality and by using Discipline to follow your dreams.

9:00 a.m. PST Clearlake, California Post Office Parking Lot

Shortly after Deborah and I were married, Bob offered us what he said was, "The best wedding gift and the best beginning to a marriage that he and Linda could offer." It was a one-week trip to The High Valley Ranch in Northern California. We were only told that it was so exclusive that no one got to just drive onto the property, so exclusive we had to meet at a certain time at the local post office to be guided in. Bob said, "Mine's the red suite and I'll bet they'll give you the red suite because of all the work I have done with them over the years."

We had visions of a luxurious resort where for one entire week we would be totally pampered in a spa-like environment. We packed our belongings into one suitcase for easy transport and brought a bottle of champagne to celebrate. When we showed up at the designated location, there were a lot of other people in the parking lot also waiting to be escorted in. I thought, "It must be a big ranch." Eventually a guy showed up and, after taking our names, we all followed him in our vehicles. Once in, the same guy took us to a staging area near some large barns and said, "Look, you have ten minutes to get your stuff unpacked." It felt like we were at boot camp. Deborah said, "This is just like when I joined the police academy."

He obviously didn't know who we were so I went over to explain that we were guests of Bob and Linda Proctor and that we were on our honeymoon. "I know exactly who you are," he said and then laughed. It turned out that my mentor's gift was a seven-day intense personal growth retreat, complete with physical obstacle courses and daily group workshops. Wait, it gets worse! The women and men were placed in separate barracks for the entire week. I will never forget the look on Deborah's face!

I quickly shoved my stuff into a garbage bag and Deborah took the suitcase. We left the champagne in the car. The others looked at us in amusement. I said to myself, "Who does this on their honeymoon?" I had to draw on everything my mentor had taught me just to stay through the first half hour. We just had to trust the process and trust Bob. We also had to learn to trust ourselves.

Bob's Handwritten Coaching Comment

I knew the best way for William and Deborah to start their life together was go to PSI SEMINAR RANCH. They really learned to live...

"I've come to trust not that events will always unfold exactly as I want but that I will be fine either way. The challenges we face in life are always lessons that serve our soul's growth."

- Marianne Williamson

This Wedding Gift Had its Ups and Downs

During the next seven days, we had to complete several different obstacles courses. We had to climb a forty-foot pole; stand up on a fourteen-inch wobbly plywood cap that spun freely and then jump out to grab a swinging trapeze bar. Three team members stood on the ground holding ropes connected to my harness — were they really paying attention? Once when the pole began swaying back and forth I yelled at the team counselor, "Stop shaking the pole!" He yelled back, "It's not the pole, it's you! Calm your mind and you will calm your body!" Excuse me, calm my mind?

One morning before daybreak, a group of us were blindfolded and led through what seemed like an uphill obstacle course. After more than an hour of ascending, our blindfolds were removed and we witnessed a spectacular California sunrise from a mountain peak several thousand feet above sea level! As I took in the sunrise I couldn't help but wonder, "Where were the others and more importantly, where was Deborah?" I hoped she was okay. Thank goodness I didn't know the truth! She was participating in an exercise in which she had to lean over a cliff with just a harness and a rope to secure her. They told her not to fear the cliff or the thousand-foot drop to jagged rocks below — just to put her trust in the counselor holding the other end of the rope; a person that she had met only minutes earlier!

It Takes a Village to Raise a William

The day after the sunrise hike, we broke into groups of fourteen and were instructed to scale an eighteen-foot wall without ropes, ladders, or climbing aids. We could, however, use each other. I am six foot-six. I looked around at the others and thought, "This will never happen." Not only were most of the others vertically challenged, they were middle-aged and somewhat paunchy. Two cars were positioned at a 45-degree angle to the wall. When I asked what the cars were for, the counsellor said, "Most groups don't make it over the wall before the sun sets so the car headlights are needed to light up the wall. When I mentioned dinner, the counsellor replied, "When the last person makes it over the wall, then we chow." It was already 5:00 pm.

We all made it over the wall, including me weighing in at over 250 lbs. I am still amazed at how we all came together to get it done. We were exhausted and even though it was very dark at the conclusion — what a celebration! But I guess they figured that the physical torment wasn't enough; we were then instructed not to speak to anyone for the next twenty-four hours! Absolutely no talking in a crowd of one hundred people! That might sound simple enough but it required an extreme amount of discipline to make it through and it just became more and more difficult as the day wore on.

Somehow Deborah and I both made it through that week. It required more discipline, physical stamina, and perseverance than I thought I was capable of. Within fifteen minutes after we left the ranch, my cell phone rang. Bob's first comment was, "How was your honeymoon?" He laughed heartily during the debriefing and then said, "If your marriage can survive that week in its first six months, then your marriage can survive anything for decades to come."

"Study and discipline are the prerequisite to any form of accomplishment. Unfortunately, studying is much like paying taxes for most of us - we only do it when we have to. If you're serious about developing greatness in your life, study the lives of great men and women and follow their advice!"

- Bob Proctor

Freedom is a Disciplined Lifestyle

I think everyone views the word *discipline* with at least some apprehension. It is synonymous with hard work, which is what this is. Because discipline not only involves the work you do, it also pertains to the life you lead. Have you considered that what you do is not nearly as important as what you don't do?

It is certainly no stretch to say that one of the biggest complaints people have today is stress. It is also fair to suggest that most of their stress is self-inflicted. We make bad choices, overload our schedules, do what is the easiest instead of what would be the best. So, the first aspect of a new disciplined YOU is developing the ability to say no. That's right. It is okay to say no to your friends, your family, your spouse, your children, and to anyone else. Always saying yes implies that your time isn't worth anything. You are always available no matter what hardship it places on you, your family, or your long-term goals.

To succeed, you must end the cycle of hypnotically saying yes. The first step is to sit down and make a list. Write down your current involvement with all the clubs, civic and church groups that you attend. List all the work you do after hours or on weekends for your job, all the classes, meetings, and shopping trips you share with friends, the lunches and dinners out, business trips, movies you go to and anything that is making you crazy busy:

- _____
- _____
- _____
- _____

Now look at your list. The objective is to sift through your list and cut the list by at least half. Sometimes it is a matter of trimming tasks. Do you have to go shopping every weekend or can you make one or two trips a month? Do you have lunch out every day or can you make it three times a week? Are you on four church committees instead of one or two? Wait! You don't want to cut back? You can't see how they will be okay without you? Then you don't want a new life.

"If you do what you have always done,
you will continue to get what you have."

- Jim Rohn

So Are You Ready to Start Getting Different Results?

Without discipline, success is impossible, period. Discipline is choosing to do what you know must be done, as often and as long as required. It's doing the thing you have to do (or not do) whether you like it or not.

Discipline allows you to control the course of your life. If you do not discipline yourself, someone else will. They, not you, will get to decide what they believe is best. Note: most people don't know how or have forgotten how to be disciplined or how to make decisions. If that is the case for you, take heart — this chapter is for you.

The Difference between Repetition and Skill Development

I was recently speaking with one of my young mentees. He was talking about the joy of reading an excellent book on personal growth and wanted to share the title with me. I asked him what he found so interesting about the book and how he was going to apply its teachings in his own life. He was stumped. He finally said, "I will go back over my highlights and underlines and share that with you later if you would like."

I reminded him of something my mentor drilled into me. When you learn anything of value, you have an obligation to take ownership of that information and pay it forward. He asked, "How?"

It's just this simple: transfer all your highlights and underlines into a word document, large font size; print it and/or upload it into your smart phone. Then read or listen to those key points from the book, five times a day for twenty-one consecutive days and you will be the proud new owner of that knowledge. You will own it so you can then mentor someone on the subject. You can then utilize the epic transfer of this knowledge in a *pay-it-forward* way. This is the very reason our creator gifted us with faculties that separate us from the animal kingdom.

People often confuse the effects of repetition on a single association and response with the effects of practice on the development of a skill. In learning any skill, what must be acquired is not an association or any series of associations, but many thousands of links that will connect specific habits with specific results. Whether it is dance, weight management, wealth creation, or removing deep-rooted paradigms that may have DNA levels of programing, most of us have entertained thoughts of making changes. We intend to make those changes but our minds remain ambivalent, which greatly reduces our chances of success. Even what might seem like a manageable attempt at repetitious learning: a driver's license test, cramming for a final exam, or memorizing birthdays and anniversaries can prove challenging and disappointing.

Each day, set yourself the task of deliberately withdrawing your attention from the objective world. In other words, concentrate on those thoughts or moods that you deliberately determine. As you focus your attention, those things that now restrict you will fade and drop away. The day you achieve control of the movements of your attention in the subjective world, you are the master of your fate. You will no longer accept the dominance of outside conditions or circumstances. You will not accept life based on the world. Having achieved control of the movements of your attention, you will assert the supremacy of imagination and put all things in subjection to it. Everything of value requires care, attention, and discipline. It always comes back to attention and repetition.

Aristotle commented on the role of repetition in learning by saying, "It is frequent repetition that produces a natural tendency."

Translation: Development is the result of repeated patterns!

Focus Requires Discipline

A large part of my past had to do with my education or to take it to a finer point, my lack of education. I spent a semester in Community College with a grand expectation of becoming a General Forester with the U.S. Forest Service. During the three-month curriculum of mapping and surveying, I concluded that I had a learning or attention disorder. I could not take a higher education path because I couldn't focus. I started to assume that I wasn't able to learn at the speed or depth required for university level courses. When I began coaching and mentoring, I heard the quote, "Repetition is the mother of all learning." So, as I applied repetition to my lessons, I got better and better at focus and at learning.

Repetition is perhaps the most intuitive principle of learning, and it is nothing new. It is traceable back to ancient Egyptian and Chinese teachings and records dating back to 3000 BC. And it certainly was nothing new to my mentor. One day, Bob handed me a one-page lesson entitled 'Responsibility' and told me to read it ten times a day for thirty consecutive days. He instructed me to put a mark on the back page for every day I read it the ten times and to call him when I had completed the assignment. I said I would, but I was doubtful. He called after a week and asked, "How is it going, William? Are you reading it ten times a day?" I told him it was going great and, "Of course I'm reading it ten times each day!" I was lying and he knew it.

That simple act of self-discipline was the most difficult thing I had ever attempted in my life to that point and it was really a tell-all to my ignorance. I finally came clean with Bob about not doing what I had committed to achieve. His response to me was, "Where else is this lack of discipline showing up in your life, William?" I could have just said, "absolutely everywhere" because that was the truth. It took me over six months to complete the task of reading that page three hundred times within one continuous thirty-day stretch. That was more than a decade ago. I continue with readings each morning — not because someone is telling me to but because I want to. I have seen the benefits spill over into every area of my life, including my thoughts, my attitude, and my behavior.

Bob's Handwritten Coaching Comment

DISCIPLINE was one of the most difficult lessons William had to learn but certainly the most valuable. DISCIPLINE is the ability to give yourself a command and then follow it ... B

"When you make a decision, you flip your brain onto a different frequency, and you will begin to attract whatever is on that frequency."

- Bob Proctor

CHANGE YOUR THOUGHTS

Self-discipline Begins with Mastery of Thought

If you don't control what you think — you can't control what you do. Simply put, self-discipline enables you to think first and act afterword.

Here is what you need to understand deep within your innermost self — your time can define your future. You think that people and organizations can't function without you – not true! And if you don't carve out time for you and your plan, you will end up in this same spot next year and the year after that. I'm not saying don't be involved, but I am saying use moderation. Perhaps your new self wants better things and you need to go back to school at least two nights a week. You can carve out the time. Be honest, but firm, with the people you normally hang with on those nights. Most of the time they will understand and be supportive. I've learned not to assume that someone will think less of me because I'm unavailable. You might be surprised at how they get on without you, which leaves you the necessary time to work on yourself and your life.

"Discipline is so basic, it's so simple and it's so misunderstood that most people go through their entire life never enjoying what they desire because they lack discipline"

- Bob Proctor

CHANGE YOUR ATTITUDE

The Mind is an Attribute of the Individual

All progress, all fulfillment of desire depends upon the control and concentration of your attention. Attention may be either attracted from without (objective) or directed from within (subjective). Attention is attracted from without when you are unconsciously occupied by whatever is in your immediate environment. The lines on this page are attracting your attention from without.

Your attention is directed from within when you deliberately choose what you will be preoccupied with mentally. What may not be so obvious is that in the objective world your attention is not only attracted *by* external stimuli it is constantly directed *to* external impressions. In this state of being, attention is usually the servant and not the master – the passenger, not the navigator of your world. There is an enormous difference between attention directed objectively and attention directed subjectively; the capacity to change your future depends on the latter. When you are able to control the movements of your attention in the subjective world you can modify or alter your life as you please. But this control cannot be achieved if you allow your attention to be constantly attracted to things outside yourself.

CHANGE YOUR BEHAVIOR

Repetition IS the Mother of All Learning

The role of repetition in constructive learning can be seen in the way we relate a new experience to a previous experience. In most everyday learning, people can achieve a close approximation of a new behavior by modeling. That method is enhanced by using self-corrective adjustments on the basis of the information feedback from a mentor.

"As a single footstep will not make a path on the earth, so a single thought will not make a pathway in the mind. To make a deep physical path, we walk again and again. To make a deep mental path, we must think over and over the kind of thoughts we wish to dominate our lives."

- Henry David Thoreau

MENTOR'S MESSAGE

By January of 2015, Deborah and I decided to change where and how we lived. Most people reach their seventies or eighties before they start to downsize, sell their home and move to a warmer climate to outlive their money. We decided we didn't want to wait until we were seventy or eighty to make such a change. We decided we were done with cold winters and that we wanted to live in Australia during the U.S. winter, which is an Australian summer, and then back to America for the summer. Year-round warmth, what a concept! We had decided and now it was time to act. After decades of accumulating stuff, we got rid of our 4,000-square foot home, the guest house and all its contents, the ranch in Idaho and all the stuff that we had collected to keep it maintained. We held garage-sales every weekend and hauled truckloads of stuff to homeless shelters or goodwill. I kept asking myself, "How is it possible to have so much stuff and why hadn't I taken an inventory of our stuff years earlier?" The accumulation was just ridiculous: I had twenty-nine screwdrivers, dozens of pliers, three drills, four hammers, and much more. Sure, I had been in the construction business but no one needs twenty-nine screwdrivers! It was so excessive, so wasteful. I wondered why I hadn't shown more discipline collecting and misplacing all of this junk.

And now for the million-dollar question: why didn't I exercise more discipline in culling through all of this trapped energy years earlier? It is so freeing and liberating to 'enlighten' your surroundings as well as your mind! Just taking the time to discipline yourself about hoarding is an exercise in freedom. If you want to experience just a bit of this feeling may I suggest you begin in your closet? This can be a real eye opener.

We agreed that we had an over-supply problem. We made the decision to put some excess clothing and a number of keepsakes into boxes. We decided that we would keep all of this stuff in storage and available should we ever need them. With some elbow grease and a keen eye, we ended up with around twenty boxes. But here is what I find so interesting about following our instinct to cull all of this excess 'stuff'. It has been a year since we boxed those items and I am at a total loss because I can't even remember what's in them. All of that energy-draining, space-taking, money-wasting fashion inventory is meaningless. Why do I say that? Because we asked ourselves this question, "If this stuff was so important that we had to keep it in storage, how have we made it a year without needing any of it?"

"If you want to make any significant change in your life, you absolutely must command yourself to do what you know has to be done and then follow through on it"

- Bob Proctor

WHAT TO DO / WHAT NOT TO DO

1. Are you often distracted from what you should be doing? What is one discipline you can put in place to avoid distractions – turn off email notifications, go to the library to work, set aside specific work (and play) hours, enlist the help of an accountability partner...

   _____

   _____

   _____

2. So, what is the greatest asset you own? (note: if it is twenty-nine screwdrivers, please reread the story above.) What could you easily do without so that your life would be easier/simpler?

   _____

   _____

   _____

3. What is one decision you can make today (that you have been putting off) that you will follow-up on? What disciplined steps are required to fulfill the decision?

   _____

   _____

   _____

WORDS OF WISDOM

- Learn to set targets AND complete them. Make a conscious decision to do what you say you will do.

- The most valuable form of discipline is the one that you impose upon yourself.

- Don't wait for things to become so drastic that others must step in and impose discipline in your life.

- Self-discipline is about aligning your goals with your actions.

- The more you practice self-discipline, the better you'll become at it.

- Keep your mind on the things you want instead of the things you don't want.

- When you're feeling information/task overload, take a minute to stop your inner dialogue and disengage. Improve your ability to separate the important from the urgent; improve your focus; save time by aligning your actions with what is important.

Without discipline, success is impossible, period. Discipline is choosing to do what you know must be done, as often and as long as required. It's doing the thing you have to do whether you like it or not.

CHAPTER SIX

Experience

The 6ᵗʰ Level of Awareness is Experience

Experience is when you are aware or conscious of an idea, you become emotionally involved in an idea, and then you act on the idea. You are then responsible for changing the end result. The change in the result, the experience of a different outcome, is due to you having disciplined yourself. You gave yourself a command, you followed the aspiration, and you took action to manifest your ideas and encouraging thoughts. As you begin to experience new and greater things, you begin to master your life.

11:00 a.m. PST San Diego, California Federal Court House

I, and two of my former partners, were being sued in a court of law with a jury of our peers and a judge. The journey that landed us in the court room had been a roller coaster ride of emotions.

Several years earlier we had signed a contract with certain financial guarantees that were completely out of the realm of typical. The individual who insisted that this was a win-win opportunity was delusional. I made a very bad judgment signing the contract. I could easily have said that someone else was to blame for the outcome, but as you have read in Chapter Three, one who continues to blame others will never achieve Mastery. It was only experience that I had lacked. When the jury came back with a guilty verdict and awarded the plaintiff a judgment worth over ten million dollars, it was surrealistic. I am sure your immediate thought was akin to mine, "Yep, signing that contract was a big mistake."

But because of the years of mentoring I had, I knew that there aren't really any mistakes — only good decisions and bad decisions. The only mistake possible would be to choose to make the same bad decision again. Bad decisions are invaluable for gaining experience in life but I no longer had time to beat myself up by continuing to make the same bad decision twice. And the good news? I've never repeated the bad decision I made in signing that contract. And I never will. As difficult as it was, I truly believe that the experience made me a better individual.

Perhaps the most interesting part was watching my mentor, Bob Proctor step in as a mediator. Out of the goodness of his heart he inserted himself and helped settle that claim for pennies on the dollar. He claimed he did it to avoid the embarrassment and hurt of three families going through personal and corporate bankruptcy. Typical mind over matter for

Bob, but it was nothing short of a miracle for the people involved. And the very best part of this experience was still to come. I became involved in the exact situation, but this time I was assigned the role of mediator. I was able to *pay it forward* to another individual and get a settlement without all the fighting in a courtroom. There are no mistakes!

There are no mistakes when we use them as lessons

When we get down on ourselves for our mistakes, we are not really understanding the value of the lesson we are being given. The lessons we gain from mistakes are what form our constructive experiences. Those experiences teach us to make better judgments. Absolutely nothing can be a waste of time when we use the experience wisely.

"It doesn't matter how you grew up, or what you've struggled with in life, your subconscious mind is unscathed by any circumstance you've yet to live."

- Bob Proctor

When we apply steadfast discipline, and see the desired results manifest, the experience gained only reinforces the awareness of our amazing abilities. Experiential learning is 'real' learning because it opens our minds to a greater source. It becomes unnecessary to gather outside information because we know that the answers we are looking for can be found within. It is only then that we can enjoy a life of true joy and abundance.

From the spiritual seeds we plant, the life-force will bring us the ideas and individuals we need to accomplish a goal or desire. As our experience is reinforced we can elevate ourselves to new and higher levels of discipline. All these experiences cannot help but continue to raise our level of awareness.

As my mentor stated, "We never arrive at the top, we only strive." The major factor in learning and experience is our recognition that all the power and all the understanding is already a part of us. When we apply repetition in being more and doing more, the results flow easier; we realize that we have always possessed powerful gifts.

"The win or the loss, which is waiting in the wings for every person, is enormous. You get to choose which you will experience."

- Eric Hoffer

Failure is a Step to Success

Thomas Edison's most memorable invention, the light bulb, purportedly took one thousand tries before he developed a successful prototype. "How did it feel to fail one thousand times?" a reporter asked. "I didn't fail one thousand times," Edison responded. "The light bulb was an invention with one thousand steps."

When we take a closer look at the great thinkers throughout history, a willingness to take on failure isn't at all a new or extraordinary thought. But unlike Edison, too many of us avoid the prospect of failure. We shrink at just the thought of what others would think and say if we failed. Now this may or may not come as a surprise, but most people don't think! And it is the reason they are so opinionated about other people's issues. In fact, most individuals are so focused on not failing that they don't aim for greatness. Most settle for a life of mediocrity, which can also be described as 'being average'.

"To many in our success-driven society, failure isn't just considered a non-option — it's deemed a deficiency," says Kathryn Schulz, author of *Being Wrong. Adventures in the Margin of Error.* "Of all the things we are wrong about, this idea of error might well top the list. It is our meta-mistake: We are wrong about what it means to be wrong. Far from being a sign of intellectual inferiority, the capacity to err is crucial to human cognition."

To achieve your personal best, to reach unparalleled heights, to make the impossible possible, you can't fear failure. You must think big and you must think positively.

"Failure is not an option."

NASA flight controller Jerry C. Bostick during the mission to bring the damaged Apollo 13 capsule back to Earth.

Great, but How Do I Think Big?

Part of the problem is that when we think of people with a big mindset, we imagine the daredevils, the pioneers, the inventors, the explorers. We think of those who embrace failure as a necessary step to unprecedented success. But you don't have to walk a tightrope, climb Mount Everest, or cure cancer to employ this mindset in your own life. Think of it this way: When the rewards of success are great, embracing the possibility of failure is a key that opens the door to overcoming the challenges. Understanding that failure is a key, whether you're reinventing yourself, starting a new business, or allowing yourself to build a deeper relationship, right-sizes the boogeyman.

Bob's Handwritten Coaching Comment

Failure is a great opportunity to learn! I had the pleasure of watching William pick himself up and stand taller...

"It doesn't matter where you are, you are nowhere compared to where you can go."

- Bob Proctor

In January of 2004, as my separation and divorce was coming to completion, one of the most valuable lessons I gained was taking responsibility for the pickle that my life was in financially — both corporate and personally.

One day as I was paying bills, the phone rang. It was my mentor. After chatting for a few minutes, he asked me why I sounded so down. I said I was paying bills. He asked, "Do you like paying bills?" I said, "NO! Who does?" He said, "Lots of people. Why don't you hire one?" I started to laugh and said, "What do you mean?" Bob paused and then said, "Look William, I learned a very long time ago that there are many things I can do, but I don't enjoy doing them. I also learned that those things can give other individuals a great deal of pleasure. For instance, I do not like doing laundry, or vacuuming, or ironing, or paying bills. So I just attracted others who enjoy those things to be in service to me and I compensate them for their efforts. A win-win opportunity." I said "I can't afford it." He said, "William, how long is it taking you to pay your bills and how much is your time worth per hour?" Finally, the penny dropped. At that time, I earned around $187.00 per hour. I called my accountant and asked them how much they charged per hour to have their in-house bookkeeper pay my bills. The answer was $25.00 an hour. Sometimes Bob can be too right!

Bob's Handwritten Coaching Comment

William has learned you are in your best vibration when you are serving others... B

"You can't escape from a prison until you recognize you are in one. People who have chosen to live within the limits of their old beliefs continue to have the same experiences. It takes effort and commitment to break old patterns.
The only limits in our life are those we impose on ourselves."

- Bob Proctor

CHANGE YOUR THOUGHTS

Witness the Internal Changes first

While others become entangled in the changes that manifest in the outside world, you can become witness to internal changes; you will see your ability to make life better for yourself and for others; you will know that it is as easy as flipping a light switch. Your God has equipped you with wonderful faculties, power, promise, and possibility. Unlike an animal in the jungle, within you lies a beautiful mind which can think, create, memorize, imagine, and dream. When you apply the principles of this book to changing your thoughts and do it with repetition, the experiences you will gain will deliver amazing results. The unfolding of your true desires awaits your discipline and your practice in changing your thoughts.

You change your thoughts by taking ownership of new information through repetition. You become the beneficiary of that knowledge (new information) and it essentially becomes you. The thoughts that have been occupying your mind will be replaced with affirmative thoughts (or positive assertions) that will change your habits and ultimately improve your results.

By repeating empowering (positive) phrases to yourself of how you want to be, you will no longer be defined by who you were raised to be… or a product of your environment or experiences … you can be all that you wish to be.

Once aware, you can't go back to a state of unawareness.

Once you are awakened, there's no going back!

To practice repetition, read the following short sentence five times a day for twenty-one consecutive days and see how your experiences and your thoughts change:

> *"I am responsible for my life…for my feelings, for my personal growth, and for every result I get."*
>
> *- Bob Proctor*

CHANGE YOUR ATTITUDE

Develop an Attitude of Gratitude

Gratitude is a feeling that acknowledges a benefit one has received or a benefit one will receive. It means learning to live life as if everything were a miracle — to become aware on a continuous basis of how much you've been given. Gratitude shifts your focus from what your life lacks to the abundance that is already present.

Gratitude exposes a common shortcoming — people tend to take for granted the good that is already present in their life. I ask my mentees to do a gratitude exercise that requires them to imagine losing some of the things that they take for granted; such as their home, their ability to see or hear, their ability to walk, or anything that currently gives them comfort. Then I ask them to imagine getting each of those things back, one by one, and consider how grateful they would be for each and every one.

There is a simple exercise that can literally change your life; start finding joy in the small things instead of holding out for big achievements — such as getting the promotion, having a comfortable nest egg, getting married, having that baby, and so on. You can have so much more joy in life by allowing yourself to feel gratitude.

You don't really know what to be grateful for?

Why not develop the practice of the gratitude exercise that I teach in my coaching program? Keep a gratitude journal. This little, daily chore consists of writing down a list of ten things for which you are grateful. Do it every day; do it just before you lay your head on the pillow at night. To begin the gratitude exercise, daily list ten things (without repeating an item) over the course of the first ten days. You will end up with a list of one hundred items you are grateful for by the end of the exercise. Most importantly, you will start to notice more of the positive around you – how beautiful nature can be, the joy in laughter, how good food tastes, the feeling of being hugged or the sun on your face... Your focus is taken away from feeling sorry for yourself for how life has treated you to being thankful for life itself.

CHANGE YOUR BEHAVIOR

Write a Letter

Another action you can employ is to write a gratitude letter to a person who has exerted a positive influence in your life. Here is a chance to thank a coach, a teacher, parent, or friend. Some experts suggest that you set up a meeting with this person and read the letter to them face to face.

I recently saw a story that really sums up **The Mentor in Me** coaching. It is a challenge that was proposed by Will Bowen, a Kansas City minister. Are you ready?

Go 21 days without complaining, criticizing, or gossiping.

Yikes! To help condition the participants to stop complaining, they each wear a purple no-complaint wristband.

A wonderful outcome of looking for things to be grateful for instead of things to complain about is that you will begin to appreciate simple pleasures, things that you previously took for granted. Gratitude should not be just a reaction to getting what you want, but an all-the-time worldview.

To become a person who notices the little things; someone who can look for the good in an unpleasant situation, start bringing gratitude into your experiences — instead of waiting for a positive experience in order to feel grateful, bring gratitude to EVERY experience.

> *"Gratitude is an attitude that hooks us up to our source of supply. And the more grateful you are, the closer you become to your maker, to the architect of the universe, to the spiritual core of your being. It's a phenomenal lesson."*
>
> *- Bob Proctor*

The Power of the Spoken Word

You can't take back the spoken word. That is a pretty powerful concept when you think about it. We've all had experiences — as kids or as adults — when someone gave us a compliment or a criticism that left an indelible mark on our mind. And as most of us know, those kinds of marks are a lot like tattoos — for better or for worse, they can be with us for life. The truth is, that comments have the potential to shape our future in both good and bad ways. And sadly it is especially true for negative feedback.

A misplaced negative word can be like a fuse that is connected to a keg of dynamite. That's because when hostile words come out, they can rip right through a heart with the power of an explosive. Words can burn a twenty-year relationship to the ground in seconds. Because once hurtful words hit the air, there's no recall button to press. They're out in the universe; they can burrow into another individual's sub-conscious to cause some real damage. This is because words are tricky things; they may sound totally harmless echoing around in your head, but they can have a totally different impact as they leave your mouth and hit oxygenated air. It is so easy to just forget the power our words have on others.

> *"Kind words can be short and easy to speak, but their echoes are truly endless."*
>
> *- Mother Teresa*

Avoid the temptation to make your presence noticed; only use your spoken words to make your absence felt. My point is: those of us who coach, mentor or operate in any form of sales or relationship building, need to stay cognizant of the kind of power and influence our words have on the people around us.

One insensitive comment can actually change the course of a person's life. You have a responsibility to the people around you; to choose your words wisely because what you say and how you say it can be a game changer. This will become a no-brainer when your habit is to say everything in a meaningful and sensitive way. And it is very important, because your opinion, your advice or feedback may just have the power to change someone's life. And if you have nothing nice to say, well, then... hit the pause button and don't say anything at all.

MENTOR'S MESSAGE

I believe that in order to have a successful life, not only do we need the right coach and mentor, we also need some very special relationships around us. We need people who produce excellent results in their chosen field, like a creative accountant, a strong lawyer with a great sense of humor, and a key contact person at the bank. The bottom line is that those relationships make my life so much easier; those people free up so much more time for me to work in the areas in which I am most productive.

My most important relationship and the one that I keep learning (and growing) from is with my wife and life partner Deborah. As a cancer survivor of over ten years, she remains very open about her life and the importance of operating from a high level of awareness and gratitude. She has demonstrated so much to me about life's challenges. It is as if I can see life with another set of eyes and ears.

One of her great demonstrations in our life is the term my mentor Bob uses: *"Calm Down to Speed Up."* Deborah repeatedly reminds me of this while eating. She is always the last one to leave the dinner table; she chews her food slowly and in small bites, thinking gratitude and enjoyment with every morsel. I am more of the, "Let's get this down, the world could end and we'd miss dessert!" variety. Deborah continues to show me that life should not be so rushed.

As a veteran of the Victoria Police in Melbourne Australia, Deborah has told me countless stories of individuals rushing, texting or simply not paying attention, which would subsequently draw the attention of the police. Their rush, rush, rush lifestyle means there is no need to target these individuals for traffic infractions, they become like a red flag for the police all on their own.

So it begs the question — Why do we need a catastrophe in our life before we can see what is really important and what is not deserving of our time, thoughts, or attention? Deborah and I spend almost twenty-four hours a day together and have since the day we were married. We travel everywhere together and we have great, in-depth conversations every day. We talk about the world around us while staying tuned in to our positive surroundings and just saying NO to negativity. It is so important that you look at your current circumstances and surroundings and ask yourself a key question:

If you were to be given an ultimatum that had only two choices:

1. Stay in your current surroundings, including the relationships that are not healthy or abundant and have a short life span or,

2. Make a decision, with no consideration of what others may think or say, to take a leap of faith knowing that much abundance, happiness, and longevity could prevail.

Which would you choose?

This is where your experience with a seasoned mentor can open so many possibilities to you. As Bob used to tell me, "This is no dress rehearsal, William. This is the real deal and you don't get a do-over." So why then do we take so much for granted when we have but one go-around? It is just our lack of Awareness. Life was meant to be a journey filled with experiences, not a sentence of status quo.

My sincere and heartfelt counsel for you is to put away those childish fears and get past those experiences that you wrongly labeled as mistakes. Take the leap. Commit through repetition to develop a higher level of awareness. Enlist the aid of a mentor and coach and see what life has in store for you as you work towards Mastery.

WHAT TO DO / WHAT NOT TO DO

1. The first important lesson gained from failure is experience. Do you see failure as a learning experience? Write about one experience that you deemed to be a failure. What did you learn from it?

   _____

   _____

   _____

2. Are you careful with your words? If not, make a commitment to think something positive about an individual or situation before opening your mouth. Wear a purple elastic band as a reminder.

   _____

   _____

   _____

3. What is one decision you can make right now — that requires a leap of faith? It doesn't have to be something BIG, it just has to be BIG for you. It might be enrolling in a night class to start on a university degree; it might be deciding that a business or personal relationship no longer serves either of you. Whatever the decision is, decide — and then act.

   _____

   _____

   _____

WORDS OF WISDOM

- Experience is the best teacher.

- Our experiences are part of us. We are the sum total of our experiences.

- Our experiences are a bigger part of ourselves than our material goods.

- The best wisdom is earned through experience.

- Experience is the best material to build character and the future.

- The greatest reward is to be able to experience every day.

- You are a spiritual being having a human experience, not a human having a spiritual experience.

Always remember, we serve for a cause and not for applause.

We live our life to express, not to impress.

CHAPTER SEVEN

The 7th Level of Awareness is – Mastery

Mastery is the final level. When we operate from a Mastery Level of Awareness, we stop letting the physical world control us and begin to control ourselves: allow your thoughts to guide your world, use gentle transitions and form the needed skills to create advancing habits.

5:20 a.m. MST September 29th 2015 Eagle Ranch, Colorado

I was in the deepest sleep while visiting in the Rocky Mountains when the silence was shattered by the sound of *The Mentor in Me* standup poster as it flew off the bedroom coffee table. It had been tossed off the table as if a strong wind had just blown it from where it had been sitting. After checking to see if a window was open or if a ceiling fan was left on high, I suddenly realized that something spiritual had just happened. Thirty minutes later, the phone rang. It was my sister; Dad has passed.

The last time I sat with my father there was a sense of knowing, without any words being exchanged, that this was the last game of cribbage we would play. I knew that I should have let him win but that look he got when I was whooping him was just too priceless. When I did win he just smiled. I knew what he was thinking from the experience of being at a higher level of awareness.

Bob Proctor was the person who gave me the ability and confidence to learn and have this gift of knowing. This ability is palpable. It is something the people around you can feel. Students have wanted to have this seventh chapter, this last lesson called Mastery, first, before the other chapters. They imagine that these words and stories will somehow take them into the knowing faster. But there are no short cuts, there is no fast track, there is just your journey. And no two journeys are the same.

Without the knowing; without understanding that all things and situations are given to us as an opportunity and not as a punishment (which is the true key to freedom and happiness), you will be jostled from high to low and back again for the rest of your life. Yes, bad things do happen to good people and so we must be vigilant in our individual awareness; we must remain conscious to accept that those bad things have deep meaning and little explanation.

My father had simply reached the end of this part of his journey. Of course, I miss him, he was my teacher in so many ways and he was my friend. But Dad, the mentor, is inside of me and he is teaching you. And the mentor in you will continue to carry things he showed to both of us. Even that poster flying off the table was a message; it is so clear: We never leave before transmitting what we have learned. This is the importance of living in the moment at the highest level of awareness possible — to be what you were individualized to manifest IS Mastery.

> **Bob's Handwritten Coaching Comment**
>
> *When you know and you know that you know. You are in harmony with God's laws, no other proof is required..*

"Mind is a master power that molds and makes. And man is mind. And ever more he takes the tool of thought in shaping what he wills brings forth a thousand joys or a thousand ills. He thinks in secret ... and it comes to pass ... his environment is but his looking glass." - *James Allan*

Serenity is the Ability to Accept

I could not begin to tell you the effect that the last chapter in the book, *As a Man Thinketh* by James Allen has had in my life. It is a masterpiece of simplicity and serenity. Take a moment to see if the passage below resonates with you; even if you don't 'get it' right away, keep it nearby. As you read, ask yourself: *What does this mean to me?* A time is coming when you will be very grateful to have his words near as you reach for Mastery.

"CALMNESS of mind is one of the beautiful jewels of wisdom. It is the result of long and patient effort in self-control. Its presence is an indication of ripened experience, and of a more than ordinary knowledge of the laws and operations of thought.

A man becomes calm in the measure that he understands himself as a thought evolved being, for such knowledge necessitates the understanding of others as the result of thought, and as he develops a right understanding, and sees more and more clearly the internal relations of things by the action of cause and effect he ceases to fuss and fume and worry and grieve, and remains poised, steadfast, serene.

The calm man, having learned how to govern himself, knows how to adapt himself to others; and they, in turn, reverence his spiritual strength, and feel that they can learn of him and rely upon him. The more tranquil a man becomes, the greater is his success, his influence, his power for good. Even the ordinary trader will find his business prosperity increase as he develops a greater self-control and equanimity, for people will always prefer to deal with a man whose demeanor is strongly equable.

The strong, calm man is always loved and revered. He is like a shade-giving tree in a thirsty land, or a sheltering rock in a storm. "Who does not love a tranquil heart, a sweet-tempered, balanced life? It does not matter whether it rains or shines, or what changes come to those possessing these blessings, for they are always sweet, serene, and calm. That exquisite poise of character, which we call serenity is the last lesson of culture; it is the flowering of life, the fruitage of the soul. It is precious as wisdom, more to be desired than gold—yea, than even fine gold. How insignificant mere money-seeking looks in comparison with a serene life—a life that dwells in the ocean of Truth, beneath the waves, beyond the reach of tempests, in the Eternal Calm!

How many people we know who sour their lives, who ruin all that is sweet and beautiful by explosive tempers, who destroy their poise of character, and make bad blood! It is a question whether the great majority of people do not ruin their lives and mar their happiness by lack of self-control. How few people we meet in life who are well-balanced, who have that exquisite poise which is characteristic of the finished character!

Yes, humanity surges with uncontrolled passion, is tumultuous with ungoverned grief, is blown about by anxiety and doubt. Only the wise man, only he whose thoughts are controlled and purified, makes the winds and the storms of the soul obey him.

Tempest-tossed souls, wherever ye may be, under whatsoever conditions ye may live, know this—in the ocean of life the isles of Blessedness are smiling, and the sunny shore of your ideal awaits your coming. Keep your hand firmly upon the helm of thought. In the barque of your soul reclines the commanding Master; He does but sleep: wake Him. Self-control is strength; Right Thought is mastery; Calmness is power. Say unto your heart, "Peace, be still!"

- James Allen

So here's the question:

How do you respond to situations and circumstances?

In the 2000 hit movie, *Pay it Forward,* an emotionally and physically scarred social studies teacher, challenges his young students to devise some type of philanthropic plan and put it into effect. A young boy, whose own life is far from rosy, takes the assignment to heart and adopts a *pay-it-forward* philosophy. The whole town embraces the boy's concept, and random acts of kindness become a community pastime. Though celebrated by acquaintances and the media, the boy continues to struggle at home with his alcoholic mother. The only one who recognizes his lonely fight is his teacher. This movie had such a powerful message, but I could not fully comprehend it until I began to *study* the powerful Law of Gender.

The Law of Gender governs what we know as *creation*. This law decrees that all hopes and dreams have a gestation or incubation period before they manifest. In other words, when we choose a goal or build the image in our mind, there will always be a definite period of time to elapse before that image manifests into physical results. I believe the most important thing we can reap from the Law of Gender, is that all things need time to grow; all things need time to mature; everything needs time to sprout into being.

My mentor, Bob, had shared this with me many years earlier in one of his seminars. I was physically present, but mentally checked out. Too bad for William, because as I climbed the *Ladder of Awareness* and began to strive to **Mastery**, this lesson was fundamental to just about every result I wanted to see. Here it is and by the way, I had to stop beating myself up that I didn't get it earlier because, as it suggests, there is a time for everything; we hear when we hear and we see when we see.

This law is true throughout nature. The variations are relatively small until higher laws are brought into play and that is the subject of another book. The point is that all seeds must germinate before sprouting up. All ideas need time to sprout and grow. So, all our hopes and dreams, our goals require time to gestate.

Think of your ideas, your hopes, dreams, and goals as a seed. When you plant a seed you must water it, tend to it, give it sunlight and fertilize it. If you become impatient and disturb the soil before the time is right, you will find your seedling (your idea), which had begun to sprout, totally upset. Your reward for impatience? It will now require more time and more nurturing for the seed to germinate, else it will die before manifesting. We can only guess about the time it will take for a given spiritual seed to develop, but the time it takes often depends on the energy put in to achieve it, i.e. how determined you are on getting it.

Most important is that you keep focused; never lose your focus (change your dream) or stop giving it energy. You receive a seed. You take it and plant it (in your subconscious mind), then you watch it and take care of it by giving it water and fertilizer (you keep focusing and working on it) and you see how it grows until the day that you can harvest its fruits (results). It is not ours to know *when* we will get the results we want. Because of the waiting and not knowing, people tend to give up and change their goals or stop dreaming. But in Mastery we never forget our goals when they do not manifest in the time we had estimated; we only change the ETA (estimated time of arrival) — not the goal.

"Be like a postage stamp. Stick to it until you get there."

- Bob Proctor

CHANGE YOUR THOUGHTS

Take an honest look at the way you view the world

Mastery is the gift of knowing that you truly do possess all the necessary faculties to live each and every day in a calm and serene environment.

Take an honest look at the way you view the world around you; do you make snap judgments of others based on experience, prejudice or jealousy? Popular fad magazines and shady self-help gurus would have you believe that success is about how you dress or the people with whom you associate. As important as those may be, more important is our thoughts.

"You must learn a new way to think before you can master a new way to be."

- Marianne Williamson

CHANGE YOUR ATTITUDE

Character is NOT Personality

Your desire to become a person of character starts with maintaining a positive attitude and mindset through all adversity. Positive people are simply more attractive people. You can determine in your own mind that you will begin to cultivate the habits of good character. Once you have set your mind to the task, 'practice' incorporating these traits into your life each and every day. Even making the decision to be a person of character will reap immediate rewards in your life. You will suddenly find yourself choosing to do the right things for the simple reason that it is the right thing to do. You will be on your way to becoming a person of character who dares to aspire to the level of **Mastery**.

Every day, you are being watched by other people whether you realize it or not. Even those you will never meet are constantly forming opinions of you. Positive character traits are developed; they aren't something you are born with. It is a very common misunderstanding for people to think it is not their job to build character, or that they 'inherited' everything that is wrong with them. News Flash from the other side: you don't inherit a good character! You work to incorporate the fundamentals: you create these habits through repetition because you have to 'build' a good character. And despite what you see in the movies and on TV: you cannot fake a good character, at least not for long. If you are going to be observed and judged by people throughout your day, you must become a person of impeccable character. The first step in developing a solid character is to build it on the strongest of foundations: Humility, truthfulness, honesty, graciousness, compassion, integrity, love, peace, and joy.

"A master in the art of living makes little distinction between his work and his play, his labor and his leisure, his mind and his body, his education and his recreation, his love and his religion. He hardly knows which is which. He simply pursues his vision of excellence at whatever he does, leaving others to decide whether he is working or playing. To him he is always doing both."

- James A. Michener

CHANGE YOUR BEHAVIOR

Abundance is Always in the Moment

When you hear about all the success stories and amazing accomplishments from top sports performers, all the stories have one thing in common: REPETITION. Who wasn't motivated by the upbringing of Tiger Woods and the repetition that his father created? Repetition that took Tiger all the way to number one in the world. Think about how many buckets of golf balls he and all the legends of golf have gone through, how many golf swings, how many balls struck from the sand trap, the putting green, the driving range, and all of this even before a PGA golf tournament was played, let alone won. What a lesson for us all.

Mastery is only possible when you truly apply the laws and principals that have been handed down from generation to generation. These results don't lie: from Henry Ford, Alexander Bell, Mother Theresa, the Rockefellers, the Carnegies, Angela Merkel, Mariusz Pudzianowsk, Oprah Winfrey, Steve Jobs, and the list goes on and on. These people got it — they were not the authors of it — they just learned it and applied the laws of discipline and repetition.

And yet, so many individuals still believe that their desires, dreams and goals in business, cherished relationships, and even their relationship with their God can be exempt from self-discipline. But our results don't lie: ask any singer, sports star, or world class medical professional and they will tell you about the thousands of hours and dollars that were invested in becoming top of their field.

Author and researcher, Malcom Gladwell postulates that the time required to be become a master at anything exceeds 10,000 hours. And that requires self-discipline. Do you truly desire an abundant future and rewarding results? Then I would strongly suggest that you reach out to a mentor or coach and ask the common-sense question, "What is the necessary action to take, the work that will be required, the repetition needed, in order to have the results that I desire?

"Character is doing the right thing when nobody's looking."

- J.C. Watts

MENTOR'S MESSAGE

We are mentoring the next generation whether we realize it or not.

It is my greatest desire to do all in my power, having been given the gift of wellbeing, to pay-it-forward to the next generation, to teach them these truths, these **Seven Levels of Awareness**, so that they will pay forward what they have found using repetition. My stated goal is to manifest fifteen million individuals who will participate in **The Mentor in Me** 21-Day Coaching Series. I set this goal at the Proctor Gallagher Seminar entitled 'The Matrixx' in 2015. But it is not MY goal alone. After all, the purpose of *'The Mentor in Me' is to bring out 'The Mentor in You'*. Together, with steadfast focus and the principles that have been true for eons, we recognize that fifteen million is a very small number.

What does my mentor say? Bob Proctor used the calculator on my smart phone to demonstrate his point. He said, "Reduce it to the ridiculous and this will show you how doable it is." He showed me that when the thousands who had already completed the course begin teaching what they had learned I would reach the fifteen million easily. It is a simple matter of math because if just half of those I mentored will mentor as many as they can… this will explode. It is of course in its own time, but there is every reason to believe that we can change fifteen million lives for the better. And that those fifteen million will continue to improve the lives of those around them by their example and through an awakened *Mentor in them.*

William was a student in my math class MATRIX®. It was there he committed to me to write this book. He kept his word, he is a Good Man... B

"The Purpose of the Mentor is to Lead Me, To the Mentor in Me."

- Bob Proctor

WHAT TO DO / WHAT NOT TO DO

1. What qualities do you most admire in successful people? If you need help, the following is a list of some of the attributes of highly successful individuals.

Determined	Focused	Patient	Integrity in Everything
Generous	Accountable	Passion	Self-Confident
Responsible	Optimist	Think Win-Win	The Ability to Say No
Masters of Time	Decisive	Disciplined	Have Balance in their Lives

_____

_____

_____

2. What one thing could you do to master one of the attributes you most admire in others?

_____

_____

_____

3. How much time do you devote to the perfection of what you do? This might include reading motivational books or listening to inspirational tapes; it might be enlisting a coach to keep you accountable; it could include going back to school or traveling to expand your knowledge and experience base. What you do changes with time — your primary focus might be on being a great parent or on becoming as healthy as you can be; it might be fulfilling your dreams of owning your own company... Whatever it is, write it down here. Next to it, write how much time you devote to perfection. Be honest.

_____

_____

_____

WORDS OF WISDOM

- Mastery is being the best at the craft you work.

- To the art of selling, vibrational energy is an essential… you've got to understand it.

- The secret of success is consistent action daily towards your goals. Use repetition as the pathway to Mastery.

- The greatest feat is to master one's own mind.

- Self-mastery comes from giving something away, whether that something is money, time, or a sincere compliment.

- Create a mastermind alliance with like-minded people — mastermind groups offer much-needed support.

- You can never practice enough – plan on being the best at what you do.

" You must do what others won't, commit, and stay the course."

- Bob Proctor

I have asked my friend and fellow traveler on this journey, Marty Jeffery, to write the closing chapter.

I couldn't think of any better way to end **The Mentor in Me.** It just didn't seem like there was anything I could say that would be appropriate to conclude or end this book when it is so apparent to me that this isn't the end… it is barely the beginning!

Bob's Handwritten Coaching Comment

When William told me he had brought Marty Jiffery in to help him tidy up, and complete "The Mentor In Me" I knew he was in touch with his inner mentor. We all need help, and he went to the best with Marty. B

CHAPTER EIGHT

Epilogue

There cannot be an end to this book because it was written so we all can recognize and awaken the Mentor in Ourselves. This is an ongoing process, generation by generation until the Master Creator decides it is complete. So, I won't say goodbye. But I can say this:

William Todd is one of those characters who loves to mess with you. He loves to tease and to be teased. Asking me to write the closing chapter in his book is liking telling someone in a round room to go and lie down in the corner. You could lose your mind trying to figure a way to end a book that was written with the purpose of introducing a never-ending concept. So, I won't do that, instead I will leave you with a few memories. I will tell you some of the poignant moments I have observed from over a quarter century of watching Bob Proctor (the mentor) and his incredibly stubborn student (William Todd) grow together.

2:46 a.m. PDT Los Angeles Hilton Hotel, Oct 17, 1999

A mutual friend and business associate, Michael DiMuccio, had convinced me that (my fear of earthquakes aside) I just wasn't important enough to invoke a quake just because I was coming to L.A. His argument was compelling. I understood that I had to get over my fear of earthquakes so I booked a room at the Los Angeles Hilton.

Michael was wrong!

A 7.0 earthquake struck southern California in the early hours of the morning, knocking an Amtrak passenger train off its tracks and damaging two highway bridges. It began with what sounded like small bugs hitting our thirteenth-floor hotel bedroom window. It woke me and my wife up. "What is that sound?" she said. "That my dear is the sound of an earthquake!" I said hoping God didn't really mean it. With the words barely out of my mouth, we were thrown onto the floor and then toward the large hotel room windows. The shaking went on for what seemed like an eternity to a Canadian 'prairie chicken' who was born on the largest, safest, tectonic plate on earth. It was all new and totally confusing. "What do you crawl under again?" In a hotel room, there isn't much to crawl under or hold on to as we stood up and then fell, stood up and fell again. We were totally amazed except for the fact that we actually thought we were dying. It was comedy at its best with fall after fall and nothing to hold on to.

Locals in Los Angeles don't take a great deal of notice of earthquakes I'm told, they are mostly annoyed because they have to reset the clock and what we called in that day, the VCR. Once we had crawled to the door and the really bad tremors were over we headed into the hallway and down the stairs. Others, who like ourselves had never been in a quake before, were freaked out. There was damage in the stairways; we had no idea if the worst had passed. When we finally made it to the lobby of the hotel, there he was — Bob Proctor with his hair just perfect; I am pretty certain he had ironed his expensive pajamas before coming down. He was busy consoling a group of people gathered around him. The group, which included the singer Kenny Rogers, was mesmerized as Bob spoke of his trust in the order of the Universe and the Law of Attraction. (Bob can hold an audience and loves speaking; I was once told that if he was awakened in the night because the refrigerator door had opened, he would feel compelled to give a talk because he saw that the light had come on.) There are no words to console a person experiencing their worst fear, however, so I didn't join Bob's impromptu seminar. In fact, I think my wife and I set a world land-speed record reaching LAX and the first flight back to the Great White North.

I share this story because the image of Bob so totally together and full of faith has never left me. Here was someone 'Walking the Talk' so to speak. He was more concerned with helping others than for his safety. He believed what he taught (and that was refreshing given the rash of false prophets that were occupying the airwaves back in that day).

Since then, my life took a turn, another one of seismic proportions.

My wife, Kari, and I were blessed with a child when I was fifty-five years old. I had no idea that old people could still reproduce. I'm kidding. I was thrilled, here was my opportunity to do fatherhood right. This was a real-life do-over. I have three adult children who, at the time, ranged in age from twenty-six to age thirty. The twenty-six-year-old was herself a mother and believe me when I say that that was one of the weirdest telephone calls ever—the day I told her she was getting that new little brother she had requested as a kid. I don't think I was a bad dad to the older kids but they were victims of my success. I didn't have a mentor to guide me in my business or in my personal life. I did it all on my own and my family suffered because I was either away or too busy all of the time. I often wonder what I could have been to my children with a bit of honesty from a mentor.

And, just for the record, if you are older and planning a child, let me mentor you on this: People will think your son is your grandson. It happens with amazing regularity. On a walk—with Luca in his stroller— a woman (about my age) approached me and said, "Oh my, what a beautiful boy. What is your grandson's name?" "Declan," I replied and she said, "Hello Declan!" I said, "His name is Luca." "But you just said your grandson's name was Declan!" she snapped, quite put-off by my stupidity. "My grandson's name is Declan; this is my son, Luca." "Oh," she said, "Oh … Oh … Oh?" The look on her face was priceless.

Having Luca turned my world upside-down. I had been saying at podiums all over the world that I really regretted not being a better and more involved father to my three eldest children. Luca was my chance to do things right. Kari suffered from severe post-partum depression after Luca's birth so I left my career; I walked the floor; I changed diapers—I acted like a real dad. I chose Luca and my family over my business, which was the right choice. It was great!

It was not great, however, for business. Except for some consulting, I was forgotten by my business peers. Truth be told, I really wasn't very good when I did work because it wasn't a passion anymore. So, I was surprised when William called me to discuss a consulting job for him and a group of leaders at our old company. The William Todd I knew back in the day and this guy were two different people. I could tell from the questions he asked and the way that he asked the questions that some massive shift had taken place. I interrupted the interview to ask a totally unprofessional question, "What happened to you, William?" He told me that Proctor had performed some mentoring voodoo on him and he was a new man.

Bob Proctor, like myself, is a Canadian. We were never friends like William and Bob are friends but Bob and I had many acquaintances in common; we had similar interests, and we were both as Bob often says, "virtually unscathed by formal education." I quietly witnessed Bob's huge success in that little movie that became a global phenomenon, *The Secret* and I saw him interviewed on shows like *Ellen* and *Larry King*. I would hear about Bob from time to time but it wasn't until I reconnected with William that I really 'got' who Bob was—until I actually grasped the concept of mentoring. Still I couldn't get my head around the change in William, so I called a number of mutual acquaintances and they all agreed. They said Proctor's mentoring (along with William's new wife, an ex-cop from Australia) had totally changed him.

If it looks like a duck, it's a duck

As we all know, things change. Luca is now ten. I am sixty-five years old. I have, as mother used to say, "Been to the beach with the boys before." I was ready for a challenge. But a book on mentoring? Why this?

I work a program in my life that teaches me to: Pause, Ask, and Remind myself that God is running the show. The reason it was 'this' is because I needed to see what real mentoring could achieve. I needed to comprehend the good, which is inherent in all of us; I needed proof that good can become the most important driving force in a person's life. I need to rediscover the mentor in me.

But I could not just accept as fact what someone 'says' is the truth without some research. And with William, I needed a 'face the earthquake in your pajamas moment' before I would totally believe this metamorphosis. And I got just that. Throughout this book, William has told on himself. He has placed himself in some very unlovely situations because that is how we grow — *in adversity is born greatness*. But my head kept saying that this was old news and I needed to see the timber of this guy in real time, now. Looking back, and given the laws we are taught in this book, I was practically asking for something bad so I could pass judgment. Sadly, that did finally happen. I recently stood beside William and watched as powers out of his control eviscerated his business, his income, and the trust that was built over twenty years of service to an ideal. There were many calls and many conversations, which went right to the brink of the old behaviors but in the end, the mentoring prevailed. He committed to help where he could. He committed to not being or doing anything negative. He turned his focus to helping others who were also overcome in this crisis.

Society loves to honor the lone wolf, but I am now convinced that a mentor is far more powerful in effecting meaningful change, repeatable change. It has been interesting to watch Bob, the elder statesman, feed William the principles needed at just the right time. It is inspiring to see the relationship between Deborah and William develop and grow. Here is a guy (who was previously incapable of this kind of union) actually demonstrating the power of a primary relationship; the power of love. Now before someone runs to the Pope with a request to have William sainted — there is still work ... just saying. But he has grown and this book, the wisdom contained in its pages, the way William has handled life's challenges... is evidence.

This book is, in many ways, like a movie; like watching the Chief Architect mold and proof his creation. Yet society has disenfranchised our seniors, our teachers, and our elders. Never before have we been so disconnected and never before have we so needed a mentor's wisdom and guidance to help us successfully handle life's challenges.

Take what is being offered in this book into your life, because without a wisdom-bank, your business and personal life will inevitably suffer. Having the wisdom of a mentor is a crucial part of your growth. And we— you and I—will never be done growing because, as we grow, life just keeps getting more expansive and better.

A Final Word — Discipline

Recently, William and I visited Bob and Linda Proctor in Bob's backyard production studio. I have worked in television stations that would love to have a facility like this. It is state-of-the-art; Bob has more toys than even the most erudite geek. Here, Bob mentors people the world over; one-on-one, in groups, at sold-out venues, and in space-age chat rooms.

Bob's mentor, Earl Nightingale could not have imagined this incredible teaching platform in Bob's backyard, where the pool pump house used to be. Earl would be pleased to see his student reaching thousands each year and millions over a lifetime. Bob does it because he 'has' to do it. He couldn't stop mentoring even if he wanted to — this is what it means to find your passion. I'm certain Bob has a number of mentees; I'm equally sure they are committed to this work. But I think Bob will tell you himself that a favorite son, a once belligerent pupil, and a non-stop source of amazement, is embodied in William Todd.

The very best moment during that entire visit for me, however, was when Bob pulled me aside and said, with his eye twinkling, "Fifty years ago, a mentor told me that discipline is when you give yourself an order and then you follow it. Everything I am, and everything you see here is because of that one statement."

Nice!

I knew he was telling me in a very kind way to get back to work, to apply some of that discipline that made me a success in the first place. And he is right.

And here is what I say to you as your new friend — go back to Chapter One and read through to Chapter Seven again and again. Make notes on what you didn't 'get' the first, and second, and third time through. There are quotes and stories from some of the best mentors on Earth. Their lessons are now yours to use and to pass on. As Bob told William, "The Purpose of the Mentor is to Lead Me, To The Mentor in Me."

Marty Jeffery

About the Author

William Todd is a self-made entrepreneur with over twenty years of expertise in the direct selling and personal development industries and a lifetime of experience in business startups. William is a protégé of Bob Proctor who was featured in the global phenomenon movie *The Secret* and is widely regarded as one of the pioneer masters and teachers of *The Law of Attraction.*

After discovering that mentors could help him achieve his goals in less time than it would take him to figure it all on his own, William created a 21-Day Coaching Program to help people of all ages and demographics (young adults, corporate executives, stay-at-home parents, retirees, and budding entrepreneurs alike) gain a higher level of awareness and improve their results in every area of their life.

William takes a unique and efficient approach to coaching by helping individuals unlock their potential through a process of eliminating old paradigms and habits. Reaching our true potential requires a formula of disciplined repetitive learning just as a gym membership requires self-discipline and repetitive workouts for optimal physical health. After twenty years of being mentored by a legend, and after a lifetime of wild successes often followed by dismal failures, William has discovered the key to that formula. William continues his mission of inspiring people to discover a new way of life through recognizing and sustaining the Five Key

Areas of Health and Wealth — Healthy Mind, Body, Family, Community, and Finances.

William has personally mentored thousands of entrepreneurs, corporate leaders, and individuals from every walk of life in over twenty countries around the world. He is the author of the *The Mentor In Me, WHAT TO DO, WHAT NOT TO DO*. The book contains lessons offered from his mentor, Bob Proctor and lessons learned from William's entrepreneurial and personal experiences. It highlights a story that is familiar to most people—being given incredible insight and guidance, but not always choosing to listen to it. *The Mentor In Me* follows the roller-coaster ride of what happens when you accept counsel from a mentor and the consequences for not. The book offers a solution for getting off the roller-coaster.

William met his Australian wife when he took a leap of faith to overcome his fear of heights by climbing the Sydney Harbour Bridge. Today, William and Deborah enjoy traveling the globe and giving back to society by sponsoring entrepreneurial teens and young adults who seek a higher level of awareness along with a better way to become global citizens. Wherever they travel, they head out and explore — taking in the culture and meeting new people. Most of what they do involves mentoring in one form or other. They are focused on helping people of all ages live a lifestyle similar to the one they are privileged to enjoy!

Bob Proctor

Featured in the blockbuster hit, *The Secret*, Bob Proctor is widely regarded as one of the living masters and teachers of The Law of Attraction and has worked in the area of mind potential for close to fifty years. He is the best-selling author of You Were Born Rich, and has transformed the lives of millions through his books, seminars, courses and personal coaching.

Proctor is a direct link to the modern science of success, stretching back to Andrew Carnegie, the great financier and philanthropist. Carnegie's secrets inspired and enthused Napoleon Hill, whose book, *Think and Grow Rich,* in turn inspired a whole genre of success philosophy books. Napoleon Hill, in turn, passed the baton on to Earl Nightingale who has since placed it in Bob Proctor's capable hands.

Proctor's wide-ranging work with business and industries around the world reads like a "who's who" of some of the largest companies in the world: Prudential Insurance, Procter and Gamble, Metropolitan Life Insurance, Royal Doulton, United States Steel, to name a few.

He has pioneered breakthrough work in the area of the mind and paradigms, prompting Dr. John Mike to assert, "I spent four years in medical school and five years in psychiatric training that included a two-year fellowship in Child and Adolescent Psychiatry. I have learned more through Bob Proctor and his teachings about the unconscious or sub-conscious mind than in all my years of training."

At 82, Proctor is a living testament to his own sage advice: we don't need to slow down, we need to calm down. His company, the Proctor Gallagher Institute is headquartered in Phoenix, AZ and operates globally.

For more information on Bob Proctor
Contact Gina Hayden
519-927-3200
gina@proctorgallagher.com

Proctor Gallagher
INSTITUTE

Marty Jeffery

Marty Jeffery is a forty-five-year marketing veteran. He began his career as a broadcaster until his entrepreneurial core eventually led him to leave the stability of a great career to become the owner and publisher of several periodicals and the co-founder of a nationwide franchise. His subsequent success gave him the opportunity to work with a large British-based corporation which was introducing a new broadcasting technology to the United States. As president of a division of the corporation, Marty was ushered into the world of regulation and the impact of lobbies in Washington. His business, corporate, and regulatory experience was the raw material from which he later drew on to create global strategies and practical training systems for several diverse world-class corporations.

Marty's corporate and entrepreneurial background also prepared him to speak before large audiences across North America and Europe. His sense of humor and extensive business experience prompted Bob Proctor to suggest he write a book called, *Laughing All the Way to the Bank*.

Marty's interest in William Todd began after witnessing the profound change William underwent while being mentored by Bob Proctor. The very fact that William became a great business leader and the author of a book on Mentoring is proof that repetition of good actions can effectively change and, in some cases, create a person's character. And as William will now tell you, nothing is more important than a good character.

Marty's business acumen and entrepreneurial experience contributed greatly to *The Mentor in Me.*

Today Marty focuses his energies on strategic design and marketing for integrated leading-edge technology groups while still personally mentoring individuals, some of whom have been with him for over forty years.

Marty is the father of four children and lives in Richmond, British Columbia with his partner of fourteen years, Kari and their ten-year-old son, Luca.

Early 2006 — The High Valley Ranch in Northern California

This Wedding Gift Had its Ups and Downs

Flight from Toronto to the U.S

Mentor + Mentee

William & Deborah gifted the custom-made redwood "PROCTOR
STUDIOS" sign from 'The Redwoods National Park - Northern California.

Dinner with Bob - The Grill On The Alley, Beverly Hills

Sorrel River Ranch Resort Leadership Event

Deb Victoria Police

To find about Mentoring Programs and Training:
www.thementorinme.com